THE IRONBOUND

An Illustrated History of Newark's 'Down Neck'

Edward A. Jardim

Stone Creek Publications

Frenchtown, New Jersey

A plat from the 1912 *Atlas of the City of Newark, New Jersey*, with the Ironbound District clearly labeled.

Stone Creek Publications
c/o Gattuso Media Design
P.O. Box 481
Frenchtown, NJ 08825
gattusomediadesign.com

ISBN: 978-0-9656338-6-4

Library of Congress Control
Number: 2016933623

CONTENTS

: CHANGING TIMES :

It might be said about the Ironbound section of Newark that, like Rodney Dangerfield – that self-deprecating comedian of fond memory – it gets no respect. Working class. Ethnic. Blue-collarish. With more than its share of factories, fumes, and funny accents, not to mention overcrowded streets with double-parked cars hemming you in on all sides just when you're ready to drive off.

Well, maybe that's not fair. The place has gotten downright respectable in recent times, a hot spot for dining, wining, and all that multicultural jazz. These days, IRONBOUND directional signs are posted ubiquitously, proudly even, in and around Newark, and the name seems to be on everyone's lips – even the New York talk-show hosts deign to mention it occasionally on their radio programs.

The place is indeed changing, but there's nothing new about that. Change has been synonymous with the Ironbound for a long time. Consider that it started out, once upon a time, as little more than marshy meadowlands, an outlying district home to just a few hardy

souls (leaving aside its Native Americans and their own hallowed history), and visited only now and then by farmers stocking up on the salt hay abundant there.

And, of course, travelers passing through. Such travelers would need help getting across the intervening waterways – the rivers Passaic and Hackensack and, if they were bound for New York, the Hudson – for which they would rely on the service of ferrymen. Thus did the main artery through the area that became known as the Ironbound get its name – "ferry road," or, sometimes, "old Ferry road." We know it today as Ferry Street. That's been its official name since the 1830s, when Newark started growing in leaps and bounds and, to facilitate all the change, the city fathers began carving out a system of streets.

Place-names like Ferry Street are central to the Ironbound saga, so largely shaped by geography and transportation. There's the Passaic River and the old Morris Canal, which helped elevate the neighborhood into industrial prominence; the main railway line that, running north and south, neatly defined the so-called

LEFT: IN 1825 THE AREA THAT CAME TO BE KNOWN AS THE IRONBOUND WAS LITTLE MORE THAN A FARMING VILLAGE ON THE BANKS OF THE PASSAIC RIVER. HAY GROWN IN THE MEADOWS WAS ONE OF THE MAIN CROPS.

"Down Neck" section – the Ironbound's alternate name; the adjacent byways and highways and various means of transit that have brought the world to the neighborhood's doorstep – historic Route 1, the Lincoln Highway, the Pulaski Skyway, Port Newark, Newark Airport.

Bend in the River

It was by way of the Passaic River, hard by the Ironbound, that the legendary band of disgruntled Connecticut Puritans came through on a day in May, 1666, to plant seeds for a new haven in New Jersey, in the process founding Newark. On that occasion, Robert Treat and friends sailed their three boats in from Newark Bay and, it has been surmised, elected to proceed beyond the swampy land of the putative Ironbound. They

---

HISTORICAL MAP SHOWING NEWARK'S 1666 PROPERTY LOTS AND OWNERS' NAMES. THE SETTLEMENT WAS FOUNDED BY PURITANS FROM CONNECTICUT.

passed the curved stretch – sometimes dubbed "Big Bend" – that inspired the descriptive nickname "the Neck." That sobriquet has been around from the very beginning of Newark's settlement, but it nevertheless fell into disfavor – especially in its "Down Neck" form – in the early years of the twentieth century, at least as far as one Ironbound clergyman was concerned. And therein lies a tale that exemplifies what might be called the Ironbound-Down Neck Dichotomy.

It was in 1905 that the Reverend John S. Allen, pastor of the New York Avenue Reformed Church, expressed publicly his exasperation with newspaper usage of what he called the "obnoxious" term "Down Neck." He was speaking at a union Thanksgiving Day service at Fifth Baptist Church, on Lafayette Street. The occasion was one of the last meetings in a city-wide religious revival, with a number of other clergymen present.

"I want to speak of a matter that has been on my mind all day," Reverend Allen said, as reported in the *Newark Evening News*. "I awoke this morning with my

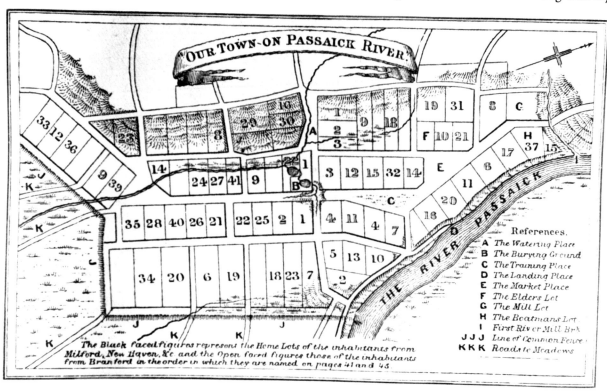

mind at peace and full of Thanksgiving joy. But when I turned to read the notices in a newspaper regarding the revival services I was disturbed by the appearance of a familiar term. At the second appearance of the obnoxious phrase my Scotch-Irish blood began to rise, and at the third I was thoroughly indignant.

"The term I object to – the fly in the ointment, the rift within the lute – is 'Down Neck,' to designate this part of the city, and my soul protests against it. There does not seem to be any historical reason for the name, nor any geographical authority, but it appears to have come about through common usage and been permitted to exist on sufferance. Our newspapers, I hope, will join with us in following the abandonment of this term and the substitution of 'East Side,' as we now have 'East Side' Park."

Reverend Allen had been pastor, since 1892, of the New York Avenue parish, serving Dutch Reformed worshippers. The parish had just recently relocated from its original site at Ferry and McWhorter streets, little more than a stone's throw from the Pennsylvania Railroad tracks and becoming increasingly crowded in a ramshackle way. The original church at the location, Second Reformed, was now a Roman Catholic sanctuary – Our Lady of Mount Carmel – serving the spiritual needs of a growing "colonia" of Italian immigrants.

"This section of Newark is not 'down,' as the spot upon which we are at this moment is higher than Broad street," Reverend Allen complained in his address at Fifth Baptist Church, "and it is not a 'neck' any more, if it ever was. Let us do away with 'Down Neck' forever." His plea seems to have touched a nerve, the *News* article suggested. "Everybody in the 409-member congregation rose in support, and the general opinion appeared to be that it would be a good thing for that part of the city."

Three days later, an editorial response in the *News* conveyed the decision of that newspaper's publishers to comply with the clergyman's appeal. "The unanimity in which he was backed up by his fellow pastors and their congregations ought, therefore, to settle the matter," the editorial asserted, "and 'Down Neck' must cease to exist except in the memory, unless people wish to flout the

THE NEWARK MEADOWS WAS AN AREA OF MARSHES AND FARMS "MORE DENSELY POPULATED BY GAME ... THAN BY MAN" BEFORE INDUSTRIAL DEVELOPMENT TOOK HOLD IN THE MID-1800S.

residents of that populous neighborhood." The editorial was titled "GOOD-BY TO DOWN NECK."

And indeed, a headline that appeared in the *News* soon afterwards, over an account of four stabbing incidents in the Ironbound – home to many Italian and other immigrants, hence, perhaps, its somewhat sardonic tone ("East Side Residents Put in Lively Day, but Without Serious Results") – seems clearly to have avoided use of the standard "Down Neck" descriptive in deference to Reverend Allen. He, incidentally, would himself be relocating, opting soon thereafter to accept an appointment as associate pastor of Marble Collegiate Church in New York City.

'Texas' and the 'Neck'

"Down Neck" and "Ironbound" have always been, and remain, completely synonymous. But by whatever name, this eastern section of Newark must have been positively bucolic as seen from the perspective of some early eyewitnesses. Especially suggestive is a brief description written long ago by a visitor named William C. Wallace, as recounted in Frank J. Urquhart's chronicle *A History of the City of Newark*, published in 1913. Depicting the territory as it appeared in the very first years of the nineteenth century, prior to the advent of canal, railroad, or the industrial era in general,

Wallace wrote glowingly: "The land east of New Jersey Railroad Avenue was in farms on rolling ground, and more densely populated by game, large and small, than by man."

Newark for a long time was little more than an isolated agricultural village, bordered as it was on three sides by salt marshes that made transportation difficult, as Glenn R. Modica points out in his online essay "The History of the Newark Sewer System." In the very early period, the common hay and grazing lands of the Ironbound-to-be were separated from the village by a fence that extended to the Passaic River, similar to the way the railroad tracks of later times were laid down to run through the area. Then, around 1717, according to William H. Shaw's *History of Essex and Union Counties,*

New Jersey (1884), "several roads were laid out on the 'Neck,' and over the meadows, for the convenience of the owners in getting in their salt hay."

Another verbal depiction of the Down Neck area in early times was conjured up at the beginning of the twentieth century by an old-time Newark resident who had spent his boyhood days there. He was William W. Morris, a Newark city official and Civil War veteran whose father in 1832 built a home on Harris Street near Ferry Street (Harris was later absorbed by Union Street). Major Morris – he served at Fredericksburg, Chancellorsville, and Gettysburg, among other places – was venerable enough to recall when this future Ironbound territory was sufficiently virgin and wide open to be tagged with what would otherwise seem a most unlikely name for this urban location – "Texas."

"The territory east of the railroad was known locally as Texas, because of its vast extent and its wilderness of swamps," Morris recalled in a reminiscence he authored for the *Newark Sunday Call* in 1901. "Few of the old land marks remain and only the oldest residents of Newark

AN 1895 MAP OF NEWARK SHOWS FACTORIES BELCHING SMOKE SOUTH AND EAST OF THE PENNSYLVANIA RAILROAD TRACKS IN THE NEIGHBORHOOD ALREADY KNOWN BY THAT TIME AS THE IRONBOUND DISTRICT.

will recognize the names of those who lived in 'Texas.'

"The names of some of the streets have been changed," Morris added. "What was Harris street is now Union street. Adams street was then known as Brick Kiln lane … In those early days [1835 to 1845] there were no tall factory chimneys to belch smoke, and the whirr of machinery was unheard. The larger part of the tract consisted of farms and swamps. Nobody thought of living below the point formed by Ferry street and what is now known as Hamburg place [later to be renamed Wilson Avenue], but which was then merely called the road to the meadows. There were scarcely a dozen streets then while now there are more than ten times that number."

Property in the low-lying "Neck" was ample and cheap before the building boom touched off by the advent of canal and railroad. In 1828, for example, some nine acres of swamp-like land in the area encompassing today's Peter Francisco Park, Ferry Street, Edison Place, and New Jersey Railroad Avenue were purchased for use as a public cemetery, a kind of potter's field, for the grand sum of $641.27. But the ensuing realization that the land would be too valuable for such use caused the opening of a new burying ground farther east, off swamp-like Hamburg Place. The latter site was used as a potter's field until 1869, after which such burials were carried out elsewhere in Newark.

Canal and 'Iron Horse'

Two events occurred in the first half of the year 1832 that changed history for Newark and its Down Neck area. In March, backers of a plan to put down tracks for a railroad that would cut through the city got a green light from the New Jersey Legislature. And on June 4, meeting at the Eagle Tavern on Broad Street, near William Street, the backers organized formally as the New Jersey Rail Road and Transportation Company, with Dr. John S. Darcy as its president. (Darcy was making quite a name for himself treating victims of that year's deadly cholera epidemic; one of the Ironbound's streets is named in his honor.)

The route chosen for the railway line was the same as that carved out originally for stagecoach travel on the old Essex and Middlesex Turnpike, now to convey the so-called "iron horse" of modern-day transportation over what would become one of the world's busiest railway stretches. The plan for this new mode of travel called for trains from Jersey City to cross the Passaic River over the Centre Street Bridge, then curve south along Park Place and Broad Street along the river, then southwest to the south end of Broad Street, and on to Elizabeth, Rahway, Woodbridge, and New Brunswick. The road adjacent to the railway became known promptly as New Jersey Rail Road Avenue, a magnet for iron and metal-working businesses ("Rail Road" became "Railroad" in later usage).

Meanwhile, on May 19 of the same year, another

historic milestone was attained with the arrival of the first boat to reach Newark via the Morris Canal seven years after it began to take shape as what we might today call a virtual waterway. The canal, conceived by Morristown's George P. Macculloch and ultimately 102 miles long, transported anthracite coal from Pennsylvania to northern New Jersey cities and towns and their iron-hungry industries, and to the New York City market as well, in the process proving to be a major economic stimulus. In 1836 it ran parallel to the route of the Passaic River through Newark's Down Neck terrain and on to Jersey City, its peak year of activity being 1866. After that, decline set in owing to competition from railroads and their freight trains.

"The term I object to – the fly in the ointment, the rift within the lute – is 'Down Neck' to designate this part of the city, and my soul protests against it."
—Rev. John S. Allen, 1905

The muscle providing the "heavy lifting" required for the canal's construction was expended overwhelmingly by Irish immigrants. The canal and the industrial activity it fostered helped spur an influx of settlers from Germany and then, later in the nineteenth century and on into the twentieth, from eastern and southern Europe, many settling in adjacent streets and alleys, and building modest homes close by the Down Neck shops and factories hungry for their laboring input.

Declared officially obsolete in 1924, the Morris Canal lives on in transmuted form today as Raymond Boulevard, designed to speed traffic through Newark – including the Ironbound – and as a bed for the city subway system.

Boomtown

"New streets have been opened in every direction," said Benjamin T. Pierson, publisher of Newark's first municipal directory, writing in 1838, three years after its inaugural printing. Pierson was referring to the city as a whole, but there was certainly building activity "east of the railroad tracks," as the area destined to become known as the Ironbound was being familiarly described. That initial directory of 1835 listed the Down Neck streets of Ferry, Market, Union, Harris, Prospect, Congress, and Elm. By 1837, six of the new streets created to cut across Ferry, in a north-south direction, were named in succession for America's Chief Executives – Jefferson, Madison, Monroe, Adams (John Quincy), Jackson, and Van Buren – and came to be tagged as the "Presidents' Streets" (in the process helping generations of schoolchildren brush up on their familiarity with early Presidential lineage). Streets would be named additionally for Millard Fillmore, John Tyler, and James K. Polk, although Tyler would later be supplanted by Pulaski.

By 1840, Pierson's street directory listed about four dozen families residing on Ferry Street, their ranks including a predominance of carpenters and agricultural growers. The properties along Ferry started with Mulford W. Casterline's grocery at 2 Ferry Street, at the corner of South Market Street – destined one day to be occupied by the triangular-shaped Ironbound Trust Company – across from the New Jersey Railroad and Transportation Company tracks and nearby ticket office. The properties extended eastward along Ferry to the farmland operated by truck gardener Samuel Richards (one of Newark's venerable family names), close to the ferry point at the Passaic River. The occupations of those listed as residents on Ferry Street included six carpenters, two masons, two blacksmiths, two boatmen-mariners, and various other craft people. There were also, for several residents at the easternmost end, addresses designated by such descriptives as "down on

LEFT: THE HARVEY STEEL COMPANY ON HAWKINS STREET, ABOUT 1891. THE BUSINESS WAS SERVICED BY THE CENTRAL RAILROAD OF NEW JERSEY AT BRILL'S STATION.

the meadows," "down Neck," "Ferry Down Neck," and "Ferry Road."

Population growth east of the tracks was strong enough by 1848 (over 4,000) to compel the Newark Common Council to carve out a fifth ward, augmenting the North, South, East, and West wards established earlier (Newark had become a full-fledged city in 1836). The new district was formally designated as such – the Fifth Ward. Among its first four representative aldermen on the Common Council were Mulford W. Casterline, the grocer at Ferry and Market. That site would become the traditional gateway to the Down Neck / Ironbound area.

Most activity on Newark's east side was centered on the Fifth Ward in the early years. Some names of note there were Casterline, Nicholas Moore, and Horace J. Poinier. Moore lived on Union Street near Ferry, was involved in the masonry and paving business,

gave financial support to St. James Church after it was founded in 1854, and also served as a city alderman. Poinier was a lumber merchant who lived on Ferry near Union and was the first of four Down Neck residents to become Mayor of Newark (1854-57).

Poinier and Moore were also among the founders in 1857 of The Howard Savings Institution, which became one of Newark's leading banks. Moore's neighbor on Union Street, additionally, was Joseph Morris, another mason contractor and a founder of the Fifth Baptist Church at Lafayette and Prospect streets. He was the father of William W. Morris, the former Union Army officer.

Different Folks

Immigrants from Ireland began arriving in steady numbers in the 1820s, some taking up farming in eastern Newark and providing labor needed for new industries. By the mid-1830s, Newark's population included about 6,000 Irish, who tended to concentrate in the eastern part of the city – Down Neck – between the Passaic River and the salt marshes. German

THE "MEADOWS" FRINGING THE PASSAIC RIVER AND NEWARK BAY ARE CLEARLY IDENTIFIED ON AN 1872 NEWARK MAP.

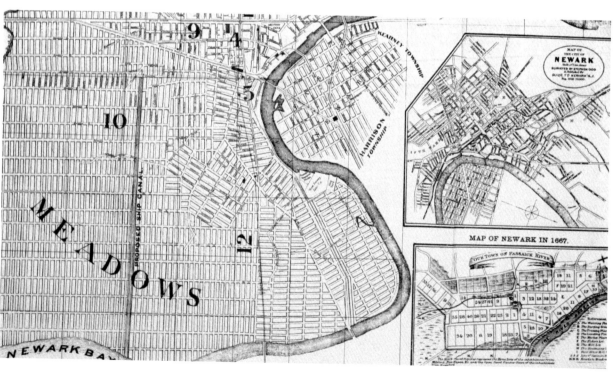

immigration intensified as well, especially by mid-century, owing to political turmoil and abortive reform movements in such states as Baden. As a result of the German ("Deutsch") influx, the "Neck" area of Newark came sometimes to be referred to as "Dutch Neck."

Meanwhile, continuing growth in population made necessary the creation in 1856 of other districts, including a Tenth Ward. It extended from New Jersey Railroad Avenue to Hamburg Place and beyond to "the Meadows." Five years later, one of the residents chosen to represent it as an alderman was Christian Wiedenmayer, the German-born owner of the Wiedenmayer brewery on Hamburg Place. It marked the first time a person of non-Anglo origin was selected to sit on the Newark Common Council.

Then, in 1860, yet another political district – the Twelfth Ward – was created, essentially cutting the Fifth Ward's cresting numbers down to equitable size. The boundaries of the new ward were defined as Ferguson Street, Hamburg Place, the Meadows, and the "East River," and its first aldermen were John Brill and Michael Nerney. With heavy numbers of Irish and German workingmen, the Twelfth Ward over the years would become known as a "Democratic Gibraltar," as the term was sometimes used in newspaper accounts. It thus represented a new political force, akin to the earlier strength of populist-minded Jacksonian Democrats, that would challenge the increasingly entrenched Republican establishment heavily dependent on such corporate powerhouses as the railroad interests.

The Down Neck-Ironbound area in its entirety would become a political powerhouse as well, rendering strong support for Democrats and other entities generally supportive of labor interests. The most lopsided vote margins were to be racked up as the Great Depression of the nineteen-thirties soured public sentiment for Republican policies. Ironbound voters in 1936, for example, gave overwhelming majorities to President Franklin D. Roosevelt and his New Deal regime. His opponent, Kansas Governor Alfred Landon, was on the short end of a citywide count of 99,277 to 37,496, but the ratio was even more one-sided for Ironbound

ADVERTISEMENT FOR A DOWN NECK MANUFACTURER OF ENGINES AND INDUSTRIAL MACHINERY, CIRCA 1912.

precincts. FDR there racked up 11,106 votes in that district's three wards to Landon's meager 2,175. In the heavily Democratic Twelfth Ward alone, the President received nearly 4,600 of the 5,393 votes cast.

By 1860, the territory east of the tracks conveying trains operated by the New Jersey Railroad and Transportation Company – and, subsequently, the Pennsylvania Railroad – was divided into three politically demographic components. These were the Fifth, Tenth, and Twelfth wards, all constituent districts of a larger entity that persisted in being known as the East Ward.

Smallest in area of the three Down Neck wards was the Fifth, which would encompass a couple of hundred acres in all. The largest by far would be the Tenth, extending south and southeast to Port Newark and virtually to Newark Airport, and the locus of a residential boom that accelerated around the turn of the century. The Tenth Ward would occupy more than 3,600 acres. The industrial-rich Twelfth, often cited as the original "Neck" area with its strong historical ties to river, canal, and characteristic "Big Bend," would come to encompass about 1,760 acres.

: IDENTITY CRISIS :

The front page of the *Newark Evening News* for January 27, 1889, contained a brief item, under the heading CITY NEWS NOTES, that stated:

"The 'Iron-bound' District Republican League will hold a meeting to-morrow night at 207 Ferry street for the installation of officers. Many well-known Republicans have been invited, and there will be a social session after the business meeting."

It was the first such use, as far as is known, of the term "Iron-bound," with or without a hyphen, to describe the neighborhood in Newark. The reference was made twice more in similar fashion in the *News* within a fortnight – on February 5 ("The Iron-Bound District Republican Club will consider the erection of a new clubhouse at its meeting tonight") and February 13 ("Many well-known Republicans and city officials were present at the first annual ball of the Ironbound District Republican League last night"). The three occasions seem clearly to have represented a baptism in print for the concept that came to be established in future years as "the Ironbound," although it would take time for the term to become standard usage.

Who coined it? Herman C. H. Herold, or so we are told. Who was he? A physician who grew up Down Neck, residing for many years on Congress Street, in the Fifth Ward, and practicing there. He achieved prominence as a public health official, was active in Republican political affairs, and served for a while as a Collector of Internal Revenue for the Federal government in New Jersey.

The assertion that Herold conceived the Ironbound descriptive was made by one Joseph A. Roney, in a pamphlet published in 1912, and we have no reason to doubt his claim. Roney was an officer of the Newark-based Manufacturers' and Merchants' Association, and his pamphlet was titled "Uplifting Down-Neck" – a title that perhaps seems at once boosterish and a shade apologetic.

Roney made the assertion about Herold in the course of taking issue with the published views of a social worker named Willard D. Price about life in the Ironbound, or at least with the tone of Price's criticism. The

LEFT: A BIRD'S-EYE VIEW OF NEWARK IN 1874, WITH THE PASSAIC RIVER IN THE FOREGROUND AND THE IRONBOUND IN THE LOWER LEFT.

latter had lamented social practices in the area which he recorded in a survey the results of which were published, under the title "The Ironbound District," in June of 1912 by the Neighborhood House. That organization was an outgrowth of the settlement-house movement, started in England in the latter part of the nineteenth century to help mostly poor urban working-class families, many of them from immigrant backgrounds, deal with the social ills and displacement that were generally associated with the Industrial Revolution.

Price was active at Neighborhood House, situated at 555 Market Street, adjacent to the newly founded Riverbank Park that was superimposed on the moribund Morris Canal adjacent to the Passaic River. At Neighborhood House venues such as the one in the Ironbound, lessons in the English language would be offered, in addition to instruction in such practical skills as dressmaking, cooking, and carpentry. Books were made available, too; the Neighborhood House on Market Street, for example, in 1902 loaned 59,215 volumes.

What especially bothered Price about the Ironbound district, based on the survey he carried out

there early in 1912, was the presence of so many saloons (Newark counted 1,200 such places citywide in the year 1890). This was in addition to what he summarized as rundown houses, dirty streets, inadequate sewer facilities, minimal recreational opportunities, and exploitation of workers. He counted 140 saloons and a supposed plethora of dance halls and gambling dens in his Ironbound survey while, at the same time, there were few churches – only four, for example, in one particular area on which he focused.

Defining "The Ironbound District" as "an area enclosed by Ferry Street, Chapel Street, Passaic Avenue and Market Street," Price said the neighborhood was so named "because it is surrounded by a belt of iron foundries. It might as appropriately have been named 'Beer Island' for it is also girdled round with a circle of immense breweries …"

"It is a curious section of Newark, tucked in east of the Pennsylvania Station between the Pennsylvania Railroad and Ferry Street and the Bowery, with Market Street running through the heart of it. It is a district of industrial uproar, drifting smoke, heavy atmosphere, dangerous acid fumes and unforgetable [sic] odors. Its people are a hodge-podge of nationalities, speaking many old-world tongues, and making pathetic efforts to adjust themselves to their new and unwholesome American surroundings."

Price went on to identify among the area's inhabitants "Irish, Poles, Italians, Germans, Jews, a few Slovaks, Hungarians, Ruthenians, and

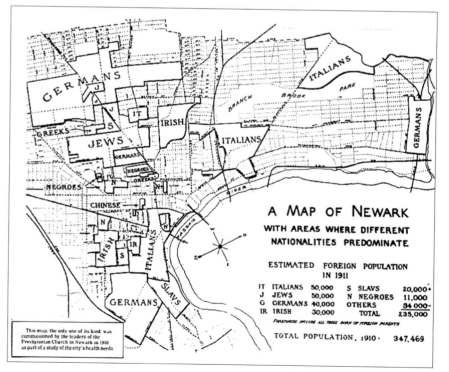

A MAP OF NEWARK

WITH AREAS WHERE DIFFERENT
NATIONALITIES PREDOMINATE

ESTIMATED FOREIGN POPULATION
IN 1911

IT	ITALIANS	50,000	S SLAVS	20,000+
J	JEWS	50,000	N NEGROES	11,000
G	GERMANS	40,000	OTHERS	34,000-
IR	IRISH	30,000	TOTAL	235,000

FOREIGNERS INCLUDE ALL THOSE BORN OF FOREIGN PARENTS

TOTAL POPULATION, 1910 : 347,469

This map, the only one of its kind, was commissioned by the leaders of the Presbyterian Church in Newark in 1910 as part of a study of the city's health needs.

A 1911 MAP OF ETHNIC GROUPS RESIDING IN NEWARK SHOWS A CONCENTRATION OF GERMANS, SLAVS, ITALIANS, IRISH, AND AFRICAN-AMERICANS IN THE IRONBOUND.

a considerable number also of 'plain Americans.' He added: "Saloons most numerous, then saloon dance halls, churches, a few gambling houses, a couple of motion picture theatres, one library and one settlement house," and he lamented the "negative influence" posed by the kind of place that would permit "close, sensual dancing." Price asked, rhetorically: "With the odds so tremendously against him, is it great wonder if he is mentally and morally inferior to his comfortable fellow-citizen up-town?"

Defending the System

In rebutting the tone of Price's criticism, Roney clearly was speaking in defense of factory owners and the interests of the business community. He acknowledged that the process of industrialization and urbanization brought about conditions that were less than optimal. "The laboring poor," Roney wrote, "were huddled together in crowded quarters above factories or were squeezed into the fringes of the meadows bordering the Passaic River and Newark Bay. This low-lying, malaria-infested area, known first as 'Down Neck' and later as 'Ironbound,' became the center of Newark's poorest immigrant settlers." He faulted some of Price's assertions, however.

"It is not called The Ironbound District because it is surrounded by a belt of 'iron foundries,'" Roney said. "This name was given this section of Newark some fifteen years ago by Dr. Herman C. H. Herold, collector of Internal Revenue, when forming a Republican club embracing the Fifth, Tenth and Twelfth wards, of the city of Newark, New Jersey, and under this sobriquet it has ever since been known."

Capitalists and social workers were frequently at odds over such matters, of course, and that disconnection is clearly reflected in the Price-Roney flap over Ironbound social life. Incidentally, one of the most eminent guests to visit the Ironbound settlement house on Market Street in those years was Jane Addams, the social-reform activist who founded Hull House in Chicago. On March 30, 1905, she had dinner with her Neighborhood House hosts, the sociologist Royal L. Melendy and his wife – progressive-minded reformers

Herman C. H. Herold has been credited with inspiring the "Ironbound" descriptive for the area otherwise known as Down Neck. The terms are synonymous and remain in common use.

from the Midwest committed to assisting mostly immigrant laborers and their families in crowded urban surroundings – before she moved on after a night's stay.

As for Melendy, a contemporary article in a national publication devoted to social reform took note of his work in the "Iron-bound district – the great factory district of Newark. This is the home of two large colonies, Italian and Slavic, the latter including Poles, Lithuanians, Hungarians and others. Beyond Van Buren street, 'way down neck,' are the homes of thousands of German, English and Irish workmen and their families. Here are multitudes of tenements of evil [sic] type into which are crowded newly arrived, unskilled laborers, neat houses of skilled workmen and few houses of well-to-do families."

It is obvious that manufacturers, too, took steps to help alleviate the pitfalls and pressures of social conditions in crowded neighborhoods – and in the process, perhaps, stem political discontent. A kind of counterpart to Neighborhood House around this time was an agency at 209 Ferry Street known as the "Ironbound Improvement Association," and a corollary group known as the "Ironbound Community House" at 136 Van Buren Street.

A letter written in 1912 by Edward B. Jacobson and published in a Midwestern university alumni newsletter seems revelatory:

Just a word from Jersey to convince you that we are not all occupied in bootlegging or fighting mosquitoes. I am still serving as executive secretary of the Ironbound Community and Industrial Service, with the Ironbound Community House as a headquarters for our service to the residents of the community as well as industrial workers in our two hundred or more industries.

At the Ironbound Community House we have seven nurses and four social workers serving the less fortunate of this industrial community. Recently I was elected to the presidency of the New Jersey Association of Community Workers. Have purchased a home recently in Maplewood, N. J.

Political Jousting

In terms of Ironbound political history, the year 1889 seems pivotal even beyond the apparent "Ironbound" coinage. Also founded that year, in addition to the Ironbound District Republican League, was the Twelfth Ward Democratic Club. Such coincident activity perhaps suggests a heating up of partisan politics on Newark's east side in this period marked by explosive urban growth and heightened social fragmentation.

The Twelfth Ward Democratic Club was formed at a meeting at Reichele's Hall, one of the many social venues that dotted the city's landscape in that time frame. Reichele's stood at the corner of Bowery and Freeman streets (Bowery street later to become Fleming Avenue). One of the legendary political figures to emerge among Democrats was the Irish-born William Harrigan, who became a Down Neck dynamo antipathetic to Republicans. Harrigan during his hectic career pushed for improved sewerage, a recreational play area for youths on Newark's east side, and, generally, working conditions favored by labor unions. Democrats were flexing their political muscles in such labor-rich urban locales as eastern Newark in these years – in the Presidential election of 1888, for example, Grover Cleveland won majorities in all three of its wards – Fifth, Tenth, and Twelfth – in his victorious bid to lead the nation as its Chief Executive.

The Ironbound had many other clubs besides Reichele's Hall where pols, patrons, and assorted ward-heelers and hangers-on mixed conviviality with politics. Harburger's Hall was Joseph Harburger's popular saloon at 80 Hamburg Place. Others in the loop were such as Bitz's Hall, Hensler's Hall, Pfeiffer Hall (on Magazine Street), St. Benedict Hall (at Komorn and Niagara streets), Donahue's Hall (Ferry and Prospect), Tenth Ward Hall (Pacific Street), and a slew of others.

> *"Just a word from Jersey to convince you that we are not all occupied in bootlegging or fighting mosquitoes."*
> —Edward B. Jacobson,
> Ironbound Community and
> Industrial Service, 1912

Innovations

There were other happenings of more than passing interest to Ironbound development in that year of 1889. For one thing, the Pennsylvania Railroad Company began construction of a new station to replace the half-century-old Market Street Depot. The new structure, completed by 1891, replaced the old island-station building that had been erected decades earlier by the New Jersey Railroad and Transportation Company. With its distinctive dark-red brick exterior and minaret-like towers, it became a favored landmark for Newark residents. It featured an auxiliary building on the other side of the tracks, both buildings being connected by a subway that ran under the tracks. It occupied space on the south side of Market Street at New Jersey Railroad Avenue across from a row of time-weathered homes and stores later demolished for a green area to be redesignated as Peter Francisco Park.

And in that same year of 1889, the growing Italian presence on the other side of the tracks – the east side – was marked by the founding of Our Lady of Mount Carmel parish to serve the spiritual needs of that immigrant group's predominantly Catholic fold. Established on December 5 and formally incorporated as La Chiesa Cattolica Italiana della Madonna del Carmine, its sanctuary was the former Second Reformed Church at Ferry and McWhorter. The fourth Roman Catholic parish to be established in the Down Neck area, its first pastor was the Italian-speaking Reverend Conrad Schotthoefer, who had been assigned by the Vatican in 1886 to serve Newark's fledgling Italian population. Their numbers in years to come would rival those of their Anglo, Irish, and German predecessors.

Originating overwhelmingly in their native land's southern region – the "Mezzogiorno" as Garibaldi had popularized it – Italians had been settling in the area centering on River Street (later to become Raymond

Boulevard) and Mulberry Street adjacent to the Morris Canal. Then, abruptly in May of 1902, tenants occupying quarters in buildings on River Street received notice to vacate the premises by June 1. The action was attributed, the *Newark Evening News* reported on May 7, to the large-scale project under way to raise the railroad tracks in the area adjacent to the Market Street Station and along the entire Pennsylvania Railroad route in Newark. Most seriously affected were Italian immigrants, who predominated among the occupants of largely tenement-type housing in the area being acquired by the railroad company.

"Where the Italian colony, at present located along River street will migrate to on June 1 is the subject of much conjecture," the *News* report asserted, "for the residents in that vicinity have all received notice to vacate their premises." In fact, many of them chose to move a few blocks east into the Fifth Ward and the heavily industrialized area along Market Street, adjacent to the Morris Canal and the Passaic River, to tenement space thereabouts. Italian workers and their families had been trickling into the area since the mid-1880s, to such streets as Jefferson, Madison, Monroe, and Jackson.

Italian labor, meanwhile, provided much of the muscle for the installation of sewer and water systems as well as railroad improvements. Eventually, the heart of the Italian "colonia" in the Ironbound shifted in a southerly direction from the congested Fifth Ward to greener expanses in the Tenth Ward and such areas there as that centered on East Side Park.

Pledging Allegiance

In 1919, East Side Park was the focal point of an "Americanization" program marking Memorial Day. It was sponsored by a group of Ironbound businessmen and manufacturers, involved many participants, and attracted a crowd of observers.

The program included a grand pageant featuring the Pledge of Allegiance to the American flag, various tableaux, folk dances, and addresses in the Russian, Polish, Italian, Lithuanian, and Czech languages, capped by a "Parade of All Nations" to Broad and Market streets at the bustling "Four Corners" center of downtown Newark.

The sponsoring group was formed in October of 1918 as "The Ironbound Community and Industrial Branch of the Y.M.C.A. of Newark," a title promptly shortened to Ironbound Community and Industrial Service. From the latter would arise, the following year, the Ironbound Community House, eventually on Van Buren Street. The latter organization made available nurses and social workers to serve "the less fortunate of this industrial community."

The aim was generally to

GREEK FAMILIES ENJOY A ROOFTOP PARTY ON FERRY STREET IN 1914. THE GATHERING MAY HAVE BEEN FOR THE PURPOSE OF MATCHMAKING.

foster adherence to American political, social, and economic values, and there were periodic visits to Ironbound factories at which instruction in citizenship and the English language was given in workplace settings. One of the sponsoring group's publications was entitled *The Better American In Ironbound*.

As early as 1907, factories in the Ironbound were the focal point of a Protestant evangelical campaign spurred by changing demographic trends and designed "to show the workingmen of Newark that the church is interested in them."

Amid tools and work benches, as the *Newark Evening News* reported in March, ministers held services that featured the "somewhat unusual spectacle" of "rousing camp meeting hymns being sung in several of the shops." The workplaces included such as the Murphy Varnish Company on McWhorter Street, the Newark Rivet Works on Lafayette Street, the Maher & Flockhart Foundry on Polk Street, and Gould & Eberhardt's on New Jersey Railroad Avenue.

Further effort was made the following year, as reported by the *News* in an article headlined "Plea Made to Save The City," in which the Reverend Davis W. Lusk of Sixth Presbyterian Church in the Ironbound noted that if the present trends continue "in a few years some of the churches will be forced to the wall or become mission stations." It was noted that "foreigners" and people of color now constituted nearly 100,000 of the city's population.

Name Change

It was patriotic fervor, whipped up by wartime furies, that caused the Newark City Commission in 1918 to abandon one of the Ironbound's venerable street names – Hamburg Place – and replace it with Wilson Avenue. The Commission's action, on June 27, sat well with the Chief Executive.

Notified of the action, President Woodrow Wilson expressed his "very deep appreciation" for the honor Newark officials rendered "in naming one of the main business thoroughfares of the city Wilson Avenue. I am particularly gratified to be honored in this way by the authorities of one of the chief cities of my own state."

Down Neck newsboys Duar Feriari (left) of 60 Monroe Street and Mike Ferinco (right) of 75 Monroe Street sell papers on a Newark sidewalk. Child-labor reformer Lewis Hines photographed the boys in 1909.

"Hamburgh" as a street name had first appeared in an 1841 city directory. In 1918, a host of alterations in Ironbound street names, as well as others in Newark, went into effect, reflecting anti-German sentiment. They included the substitution of Rome for Berlin, London for Dresden, Marne for Bremen, Belgium for German, Paris for Frankfort, Somme for Frederick, and Pershing for Bismarck.

Another switch in names that involved an Ironbound landmark occurred in 1923 when East Side Park became Independence Park. Activists within the community had petitioned the Essex County Park Commission to make the change for the purpose of instilling in foreign-born residents "a new significance" about the tenets of democracy. The change of name took effect, symbolically, on July 4.

┇ THE RAIL STORY ┇

There has been a train station at Market Street and New Jersey Railroad Avenue since 1838, when Martin Van Buren was in the White House and Abe Lincoln was still a bachelor. That was the year it was built, the first of five in all to serve as places where prospective riders would buy tickets.

The "depot," the term by which train stations of the time were normally known, occupied the northeast corner of that intersection, more or less at the spot where today's cars and buses, bound for uptown, proceed under the elevated tracks to go west on Market Street. That corner location would be only steps away from the ticket windows inside Penn Station where today's customers are served.

That first station was followed by a second one erected in 1840 "on the other side of the tracks," as one historical account states without elaboration, and a third went up in 1842 at the southeast corner of that intersection, directly facing today's Peter Francisco Park. That third version of the depot (there was also an engine house nearby) would serve for nearly half a century, until a more grandly ornamental Market Street Station went up, starting in 1889, at that same location across from the future park.

Credit for much of this early information goes to old-timers with long memory spans who left us with accounts of the way things were. One of them was William W. Morris, who spent his boyhood years near the train depots. He vividly depicted the scene from yesteryear in a *Newark Sunday Call* reminiscence, in 1901, that included a sketch of fascinating impressionistic detail. The article appeared under the title "DOWN NECK" SIXTY YEARS AGO.

Railroads initially were both a modern-day marvel and a newfangled curiosity. Neighborhood youngsters knowledgeable about such as round-houses would hang out at the Depot and over by the Centre Street bridge and race along New Jersey Railroad Avenue. They kept their eyes peeled, as old newspaper accounts report, for incoming and outgoing trains, keen on seeing their favorite "Iron Horse" locomotives as well as engineers, firemen, and conductors.

LEFT: THE PENNSYLVANIA RAILROAD BUILT THE DOCK BRIDGE ACROSS THE PASSAIC RIVER FROM NEWARK TO HARRISON IN 1935. IT NOW CARRIES AMTRAK AND PATH TRAINS.

The Depot would be the scene in years to come of many events of more than passing interest. There was the March day in 1849 when three dozen men said goodbye to family and friends and boarded a train that would take them on the first leg of an overland journey as part of the California gold rush. They were led by no less than Dr. John S. Darcy, the New Jersey Railroad and Transportation Company executive who, despite his sixty-one years, undertook the trip as a health tonic – the adventure proved to be quixotic and he would eventually return to Newark and his medical practice.

There was the sad April morning in 1865 when the funeral train bearing President Lincoln's remains, its engine draped in dark bunting, moved slowly among crowds of mourners along New Jersey Railroad Avenue and paused at the Depot. And the day in 1880 when former President Ulysses S. Grant was cheered upon arriving for the unveiling of a monument to a former comrade-in-arms, New Jersey's own General Philip Kearny.

Enter the 'Pennsy'

A key moment in railway history came in 1872 when the Pennsylvania Railroad made its entry into the all-important New York market through a consolidation of rail and canal entities and in the process began a century-long association with the City of Newark. This corporate giant known as "PRR" and the "Pennsy" went on to consolidate its preeminence as the so-called "Standard Railroad of America."

Also a factor in the Down Neck community and its development was the Central Railroad of New Jersey, or CNJ, established in 1849 in a makeover of the Elizabethtown and Somerville Railroad. It sent its trains eastward from central Newark across New Jersey Railroad and, later, PRR tracks through the Down Neck area to Jersey City.

In 1869, thousands of prospective patrons took advantage of an offer for a free train ride as the CNJ's newly formed Newark and New-York Railroad subsidiary marked the opening of service, on Saturday, July 23. Operating as an extension of the CNJ's main line for New York-bound service from Elizabethport across Newark Bay, the new line offered a faster route to the CNJ's Hudson River terminal in Jersey City.

"The passage was made from the Newark depot in Broad-street to the Communipaw Ferry in 17 minutes," the *New York Times* reported.

CNJ trains since 1864 had offered an upgraded New York-bound service, via the Elizabethtown Ferry from Elizabethport, through an extension of the original rail line across Newark Bay to Jersey City. In 1872 a branch was opened from Elizabethport on the main line to Brills Junction of the Newark and New-York line, in Newark's Down Neck section, and branches were built there to serve the growing number of industrial plants.

CNJ acquired property Down Neck for expanded rail lines and stations, with depots on Ferry and East Ferry streets and at the easternmost Newark Transfer point situated close to the Passaic River. A Manufacturers' Railroad began operating in 1882, followed by a Manufacturers' Extension line in 1889. The year 1916 brought a 1.6-mile extension from Brills Junction to the Passaic River, also for industrial freight use.

Raising the Tracks

Another old-timer who frequently reflected on times past, the popular storyteller Howard Garis of the *Newark Evening News*, commented late in life about the public clamor that once prevailed on the subject of trains coursing through crowded cities at street level.

"Down Neck begins just east of the Pennsylvania Railroad elevated tracks," Garis wrote in the 1940s. "They weren't elevated in 1896. There were man-

> "Down Neck begins just east of the Pennsylvania Railroad elevated tracks … They weren't elevated in 1896. There were man-operated safety gates which went down and up many times a day or night as hundreds of trains pulled into the old Pennsylvania Railroad station."
>
> — Howard Garis, *Newark Evening News*

Crowds began to gather on New Jersey Railroad Avenue early in the morning, before seven o'clock, on a cruel day in April, to await the funeral train bearing Abraham Lincoln's remains, nine days after his death from an assassin's bullet.

Standing mute at the Chestnut Street Depot and then at the Market Street Depot, the mourners witnessed the coming of the locomotive, heavily draped, followed by the other cars in the train procession. It was Monday, April 24, 1865.

"The tops of the houses and sheds and every available window along the street was filled with people, not excited, but quiet, apparently, with grief unspeakable," according to one account. "The train passed slowly among the people with uncovered heads, bowed reverently, many persons shedding tears."

The occasion was grimly at odds with the day four years earlier when the President-elect first came to Newark, en route to his inauguration and filled with a sense of mission for the challenge ahead. Now the backdrop was one of church bells tolling and guns being fired in sad tribute. "No sound was heard in that great throng of thousands of human beings but the faint sobbing of those unable to control their feelings."

Abraham Lincoln's funeral train.

operated safety gates which went down and up many times a day or night as hundreds of trains pulled into the old Pennsylvania Railroad station."

Accidents involving trains at grade crossings were coming to be quite a problem. Things were bad enough by 1888 that Newark Mayor Joseph Haynes called publicly for the Central Railroad of New Jersey to elevate its tracks over the city's streets, a plea promptly endorsed by the *Newark Evening News*.

In 1900, Mayor James M. Seymour asserted that Newark "is in this respect behind almost every other city in the country," and in September the *Sunday Call*

demanded that railroad companies take action. Then, in January 1901, the Newark Common Council adopted an ordinance calling on the Pennsylvania Railroad to elevate its tracks in the city, extending along New Jersey Railroad Avenue from the Passaic River in the northeast to Elizabeth in the southwest. A day later, the railroad company announced that it would comply.

Workers in mid-March began altering the location of tracks near South Street as the PRR embarked on the lengthy and expensive process of raising the rails. The project was a major concern for PRR President Alexander J. Cassatt, who visited Newark to oversee

the work. Cassatt – brother of the famed Impressionist painter Mary Cassatt – was also a driving force behind the proposal for a tunnel under the Hudson River and an expansive Penn Station in Manhattan.

Off the Ground

As a huge crowd of passengers and spectators watched, history was made early on a Sunday morning in July of 1902 when a train traversed an elevated Pennsylvania Railroad track in Newark near the Market Street Station. The deed was heralded the next day, July 21, in a page-one report in the *Newark Evening News* accompanied by photos and a banner headline that proclaimed:

PENNSYLVANIA TRACK ELEVATION A REALITY
SOUTH OF MARKET STREET FOR WEST TRAINS

"It took barely ten minutes for the gang of trackmen to move the three or four rail lengths," the report stated, and the coordinated work the laborers did permitted the westbound train to be sent over the raised track from Hamilton street at New Jersey Railroad Avenue to points south. Then, on August 5, again as a large crowd watched, workmen did the same for eastbound tracks, and all trains bound for Newark and New York could now run over the newly laid rails.

Any further debate about the urgency of eliminating the street-crossing hazard was effectively ended by a horrific event in February of 1903 that shocked the city and beyond. Nine students from Newark High School were fatally injured when a locomotive crashed into their crowded horse-drawn trolley car at a grade crossing on Clifton Avenue in north Newark. The grisly incident prompted an immediate *New York Times* editorial sharply demanding the elimination of all grade crossings.

Six rail lines were passing through Newark every day at this point, conveying some seven hundred trains with thousands of passengers over thirty miles of track. The Market Street Station was one of fourteen in the city.

LEFT: A SECTION OF THE WAITING AREA AT THE NEW PENN STATION IN NEWARK, 1935.

A New Station?

The big news on April 1, 1910, was that a brand-new train station was in the works for Newark which "in all probability will be the largest railroad station in the State." Expanded from four tracks to six, it would, according to the *New York Times* report, be erected by the Pennsylvania Railroad to replace the Market Street Station built only two decades earlier – testifying to the tremendous increase in traffic between Newark and New York City.

The report, however, was premature, and by a long shot. The railroad company and the City of Newark would wrangle interminably over financial costs and engineering complications. Not for a full quarter-century would a new version of a railway station be open for business at this vital stop along the PRR line.

Meanwhile, ideas were beginning to percolate on making over the congested area around the Market Street Station – an area showing the baleful effect, as with much of urban America, of decades of helter-skelter residential and commercial development. In 1913, a complex building scheme was put forth that would turn the area around the station into a spacious, rotunda-style "Ironbound Plaza" offering access to pedestrians only.

A manifestation of the so-called "City Beautiful" ideal then popular here and abroad, the plaza was designed by architects George B. Ford and George Post & Sons for Newark's newly established city Planning Commission. A similarly grand design was put forward two years later, in 1915, that called for a large circular or octagonal plaza surrounding a brand-new train station – long under consideration – and also proposing the construction of a new Federal postal office that would be built on a triangular plot nearby.

Several major streets, including Market and Ferry and a precursor to the route that became Raymond Boulevard, would feed into the plaza. One effect of the proposed plaza would be to provide an inviting gateway to the proverbial "other side of the tracks" – the crowded Ironbound on Newark's east side. The Newark Public Library's distinguished director John Cotton Dana, writing in 1914 in the Library's periodical *The Newarker*, envisioned such a plaza as a point of entry "to the promising eastern section,

Newark Penn Station was designed by the firm of McKim, Mead & White in Art Deco style with Neoclassical touches throughout.

A Grand Project

In a public meeting on Christmas Eve in 1928, the Newark City Commission adopted an ordinance that gave a green light to the much discussed plan to replace the four-decade-old Market Street Station with a terminal accommodating various transit systems. The following year, on November 18, construction began on the Newark City Subway in the bed of the abandoned Morris Canal, and North Canal Street, as the downtown portion of the drained canal was called, became Raymond Boulevard.

Finally, in 1932, amid a worsening economic depression, groundwork began in January on the joint public-private enterprise that would give Newark and the Pennsylvania Railroad company a handsome new station on one of the world's busiest rail corridors.

Long in the works, the project would exact much time and money – three years and a couple of months, plus forty-two million dollars. The financial cost would be split more or less down the middle for the PRR and the city. In actuality, the enterprise would consume eight years, from 1929 to 1937, before all of its component parts would be in place. They called for a main station building, two platforms and three tracks, and a new lift bridge over the Passaic River, followed by two more tracks and platforms for rapid-transit ("Tubes") purposes. Ultimately there would be a total of eight tracks and six platforms spanning Raymond Boulevard and Market Street, with six tracks on the three new bridges erected.

Then, in 1935, an even century after the trains started running in Newark, a gleaming new Pennsylvania Railroad Station made its grand debut. Length: two hundred and ninety-three feet. Type of façade: Indiana limestone and glass. Number of tracks: eight. Vital accessory: a new lift bridge over the Passaic River. Links: Hudson "Tubes" and Newark city subway, buses and taxicabs and private automobiles. Ornamentation: striking Art Deco detail, an artistically encapsulated summary of transit history embedded on the walls of the spacious main waiting room representing such as Horse and Canoe, Stage-Coach and Prairie Schooner, Columbus's Santa Maria and the Pilgrims' Mayflower.

Cost to the Pennsy rail company: twenty million dollars. Cost to Newark's taxpayers: twenty-two

whose possibilities of development are so great."

Dana lamented what he called the unprepossessing view of Newark as seen from the windows of Pennsylvania Railroad trains passing through. "Travelers on their way to and from New York thus get the impression," he wrote, "that this is a squalid and ugly city."

million. The *Newark Sunday Call* would later declare: "Father Newark started a drive for a new Pennsylvania Railroad station in 1910, finally got a station in 1935; but the long wait was worth while."

Some fifteen thousand people turned out on Saturday, March 24, for the dedication of the building, which was rendered in neoclassic design by the prestigious New York architectural firm of McKim, Mead & White. The first train actually to use the new station, a Philadelphia Express, arrived the next morning at 10:17.

The main entrance to "Penn Station," as it would become universally known, was on Raymond Plaza West, thus keeping alive the old custom of relegating the Down Neck / Ironbound side (Raymond Plaza East) to the back side, as it were. Nonetheless, the imposing, streamlined profile of the edifice gave a touch of grace to the east side of town, for a change.

Two years later, the end of an era would be reached in the wee hours of Sunday, June 20, as the Hudson & Manhattan rapid-transit trains known as the "Hudson Tubes" (and later known as PATH) slipped out of the old Park Place station in Newark for the last time. The terminus now shifted a few blocks away to Penn Station.

It was the last step in the grand project long envisioned that sought to consolidate the various means of transit at one central Pennsylvania Railroad-related location in Newark (the main Newark City Subway line, too, was completed in 1935 and extended two years later to the new Penn Station). The shift in 1937 brought a halt to use of the upper deck of the venerable Centre Street bridge, over which the Hudson & Manhattan trains rolled, and abandonment of the old Manhattan Transfer station across the Passaic River in the Harrison meadows whereby commuters bound for downtown New York switched between trains and "Tubes."

Unfortunately, the occasion was marred by the accidental deaths of two workmen who were struck that June evening in 1937 by a train on one of the Pennsylvania Railroad tracks, between Lafayette and Green streets.

NEWARK'S PENN STATION FROM THE NORTHEAST. THE IRONBOUND STRETCHES EAST OF THE TRACKS TO THE LEFT OF THE FRAME.

: By Land, Sea and Air :

Location plays a central role in the Ironbound / Down Neck saga. The place seems ringed with ports of entry and avenues of escape, with highways, flyways, and skyways. For those looking backward for insight as to how geography helped shape its character, herein are some notes on the proverbial sense of "location, location, location" undergirding one neighborhood's history.

Plank and Ferry

An important step was taken, early on, in the way of more effectively connecting Newark and New York through construction of a public road. Such was authorized in 1765 by the New Jersey Legislature.

The route, superimposed on a throughway of wooden planks first laid out early in the eighteenth century, became known as the "ferry road," predecessor to today's Ferry Street – the Ironbound's main artery. The action by the state also included the establishment of ferries at the Passaic and Hackensack rivers.

One of the more famous travelers along the route was George Washington. According to *Newark Evening News* journalist Howard Garis, who wrote frequently about Down Neck lore, Washington was in Newark on June 25, 1775, and became aware of a British plot to capture him – he had been named commander-in-chief of the Continental Army. To circumvent the enemy, Washington rode on horseback down the ferry road. As Garis recounts: "Once over the Passaic on the ferry from Ferry street, Washington crossed over the meadows to the Hackensack River. There he took Dow's Ferry and so went to Hoboken and safely crossed to New York."

The same ferry road also would figure, five years later, in an invasion by a British military contingent which then engaged colonials in a battle in the central part of Newark Township before retreating via the same route.

In 1792, bridges over both the Passaic and Hackensack rivers were erected to upgrade traffic connections between Newark and Paulus Hook – also known as Jersey City. The bridge building led ultimately to the phasing out of the ferry system.

Much later, in 1849, the archaic road bed of rough logs that conveyed horses and wagons on the ferry road was replaced by smooth wooden planks. They were part

---

Left: The Pulaski Skyway spans the Passaic and Hackensack rivers between Newark and Jersey City.

JACKSON STREET BRIDGE (TOP) CROSSES THE PASSAIC RIVER FROM NEWARK'S IRONBOUND AREA TO HARRISON. GEARS IN THE BRIDGE'S CONTROL HOUSE (BOTTOM) PIVOT THE SPAN FOR VESSELS TO PASS.

Harrison, the Hudson County municipality across the river.

Another new bridge, opened in 1904, extended Plank Road over the Hackensack River, further facilitating traffic between Essex and Hudson counties. Then, in 1913, Plank Road became part of the scheme for a Lincoln Highway that was designed as a link in an envisioned coast-to-coast route across America appropriate to the brave new "age of the automobile."

Planned to stretch from New York to San Francisco, the Lincoln Highway was opened on December 13, 1913. The first leg of its route cut through Newark's Ironbound area from Jersey City via the Old Plank Road and Ferry, Merchant, and Lafayette streets before continuing to Broad Street and points south and west.

Port Newark

The date was October 20, 1915. After a year of dredging and reclamation of thousands of acres of tide marshland on Newark Bay, ceremonies on that Wednesday marked the beginning of a new era for Port Newark, off the city's southeastern edge adjacent to the Ironbound district.

Mayor Thomas L. Raymond and business leaders were on hand for what was billed as "Port Newark Terminal Day." With funding supplied by a two-million-dollar state bond issue, the main feature was a ship channel 7,000 feet long, 400 feet wide at bottom, and 20 feet deep at mean low water, complete with a 1,200-foot-long pier. Dock frontage was equipped with derricks and tracks to handle freight, and there was accommodation, too, for rail lines.

of a new system renamed Plank Road, running eastward through the Down Neck area from the junction of Ferry Street and Hamburg Place. The system was put in place by the newly incorporated Newark Plank Road and Ferry Company.

A new span over the Passaic River opened to traffic on November 25 – Thanksgiving Day – in 1897. It was the Jackson Street Swing Bridge, directly connecting Newark's Down Neck area with

The makeover turned the 848-acre tract into one of the most active seaports on the East Coast. A headline in the *New York Times* referred to the grand project as the "Filling In of 4,000 Acres of Useless Meadows." The impulse to carve out a ship canal in this territory frequently identified on maps as "Newark Meadows" was an old one, dating as far back as 1870. Newark had first gained official seaport status in 1834, when Congress declared the burgeoning city a port of entry to the United States.

Up and Over

Ironbound residents had a front-row seat, figuratively speaking, as the sparkling new Pulaski Skyway took its giant leap into so-called "super highway" history in 1932.

It was November 24, a Thanksgiving holiday, and the public was invited to test out the imposing 3.5-mile viaduct that soared gracefully over swampy meadows and two bodies of water to more directly connect the cities of Newark and Jersey City than ever before. The bridge was costly – twenty million dollars and thirty months' labor. Fifteen lives were lost in work-related accidents.

Praised by engineering experts, the steel deck truss cantilever bridge features a pair of 550-foot spans that traverse the Passaic and Hackensack rivers. It thereby cut down significantly on the tedium previously required to maneuver twisting streets, bothersome traffic lights, and time-consuming drawbridges. The Skyway stretched from the Tonnelle Avenue circle in Jersey City to Raymond Boulevard in the Ironbound and helped expedite ever-increasing traffic piling up on Newark's eastern corridor. Six years after its opening, it was destroyed – though only fictionally – in Orson Welles's "War of the Worlds" broadcast on a Halloween night that caused a good deal of fear among the populace, including Ironbound inhabitants.

The new creation went by a number of titles at first – the Newark-Jersey City Viaduct, the Meadowlands Viaduct, the Diagonal Highway, the High-Level Viaduct – before finally, in September 1933, being renamed in honor of the Polish-born General Casimir Pulaski, of Revolutionary War fame.

Fly Away

The star attraction in 1935, as Newark Metropolitan Airport showed off its new administration building to the public, was Amelia Earhart. The slender, 36-year-old aviator who was charming public and press with her tomboyish smile en route to becoming an aviation legend, was one of some 10,000 people on hand – half of them Newark schoolchildren, turning out in force on a Wednesday afternoon in mid-May. The occasion was the dedication of the $500,000 airport administration building.

"The value of Newark Airport as a center of aviation and an air-mail base has been greatly enhanced," Mayor Meyer C. Ellenstein said, "by the Holland Tunnel and the Pulaski Skyway, linking Newark with the great city of New York." It was less than eight years since another mayor, the visionary-minded Thomas Lynch Raymond, had set into motion plans for a six-million-dollar airfield to be built, owned, and operated by the city at Port Newark.

As for Earhart, less than two months after the Newark Airport dedication, she and her co-pilot would vanish in mid-air – last heard from while flying somewhere over the central Pacific Ocean.

The End of the Line

By 1937, the end was near for trolley cars on Newark streets, including the Ironbound. Public Service Co-ordinated Transport was completing its shift to the ASV or "all service vehicles," otherwise known as trolleybuses. August 1, a Sunday, was exit date for an old line – the No. 1 Plank Road route between Newark and Jersey City.

The route of the so-called 1 Newark line traversed, in part, Ferry Street, Market Street, Fleming Avenue, Ferry Street again, Raymond Boulevard, and on to Kearny and Jersey City. Another busy line was the 31 South Orange, by which trolley cars ran for years along Ferry Street to Hamburg Place / Wilson Avenue.

Trolley-car operations in Newark began on October 4, 1890, at the brand-new Market Street Station of the Pennsylvania Railroad. After trolleys were fully abandoned, the last of the iron rails were gradually, after the late 1930s, dislodged from the streets.

NEWARK
SMELTING & REFINING
WORKS
E. D. BALBACH & SON

THOS. P. WAY

: BEER AND BUSINESS :

The so-called "Ironbound District" might just as well have been named "Beer Island," said a temperate-minded social worker, as mentioned earlier in this history, "for it is also girdled round with a circle of immense breweries. The ocean-like waves sweeping in from this open sea fairly submerge the little island at times."

Such was the judgment of Willard Price, of Neighborhood House, who reported 140 saloons in the survey he conducted Down Neck, not to mention the dance halls of dubious propriety he said he also encountered there. It would seem not an unlikely locale for taverns, given Newark's ample supply of breweries – eighteen of them in 1918, including prominent Ironbound-related names like Ballantine, Feigenspan, Hensler, and Wiedenmayer.

Two of the earliest of the Newark brewers were Johann Nepomuk Schalk and Peter Ballantine. Schalk, of Baden heritage, came to America in 1849 early in the immigrant surge that would bring countless numbers of Germans to these shores. Skilled in the art of brewing the kind of light lager beer favored by his fellow nationals, he purchased property at the corner of Napoleon Street and Hamburg Place for his business, then moved to a new and larger site on Freeman Street between Bowery and Ferry streets.

Schalk was instrumental in making Newark a haven for beer-making. Close proximity to the Passaic River helped make the areas involved a natural venue for breweries. When he retired and returned to Germany, his sons Adolph and Herman took over, operating the business first out of 82 Hamburg Place and then from Freeman Street. Herman Schalk served as an alderman on the Newark Common Council, representing the Twelfth Ward, the second of German descent in that political role after Christian Wiedenmayer.

In 1874 Herman Schalk paid a memorable visit to the old homeland, being feted at one point by the famed "Iron Duke" who was Germany's Chancellor, Otto von Bismarck.

Lager Over Ale

In 1879 the Schalk business was bought out by another beer-maker, the Scottish-born Peter Ballantine.

LEFT: THE BALBACH SMELTING & REFINING COMPANY, CIRCA 1870. ESTABLISHED BY THE GERMAN-BORN BALBACH FAMILY, THE COMPANY BECAME ONE OF THE LARGEST METAL REFINING OPERATIONS IN THE UNITED STATES.

A HORSE-DRAWN BEER WAGON DRAWS UP TO THE HENSLER
BREWERY ON HAMBURG PLACE, 1882.

Newark at that point had twenty-six breweries and was producing almost eighty-five per cent of New Jersey's total beer output. Ballantine had been in the brewing business in Newark since 1840. He enhanced his company's success by favoring lager over ale to satisfy the taste of the large German-American market.

His acquisition of the Schalk company enabled him to expand his beer-making dominance in the city. With offices at 58 Freeman Street in the Ironbound area, the newest of his brewing plants occupied land bordered by Fleming Avenue and by Oxford, Christie, and Ferry streets. Although greatly weakened by the feckless Prohibition "experiment" of the 1920s, P. Ballantine & Sons became one of the mightiest of American breweries before the Freeman-Ferry complex was shut down in 1972 and phased out in 1983.

Another early German arrival who made good as a brewer was Christopher Wiedenmayer, who began operating in the 1850s on Hamburg Place. According to one account (*Newark: The Golden Age*, by Jean-Rae Turner, Richard T. Koles, and Charles F. Cummings), Wiedenmayer's business soon grew to three buildings, a stable for thirty-six horses, and a cold storage center capable of holding 20,000 barrels of beer.

George H. Weidenmayer, who took over his father's brewery in 1879, served as a Newark alderman and New Jersey State assemblyman. He also provided a field where baseball was played, that particular sport growing in stature to an increasingly professional degree over the years, luring generations of fans to the athletic venue on Hamburg Place / Wilson Avenue.

Hensler on Hamburg

Joseph Hensler, who was born in Berlin about 1830, worked with the Schalk Brothers and with Lorenz & Jacquillard in Newark before starting his own brewery in 1860. There, on Hamburg Place, it would become a fixture for nearly a century.

Operating for several years as Lorenz & Hensler, the company became most prominent as the Joseph Hensler Brewing Company for most of its lifespan producing lager beer. Joseph Hensler served on the Newark Common Council and was a financial supporter of the Twelfth Ward German English School, among other activities. He was succeeded in business after his death in 1902 by his sons Adolph and Joseph.

The senior Hensler lived in close proximity to his workplace, the factory office being at 73 Hamburg Place while its owner resided across the street, at 426 Lafayette, in a house with Victorian ornamentation he had built for him – the site today of the Buyus Funeral Home. Hundreds of Hensler employees and friends became loyalists, in the late nineteenth and early twentieth centuries, in the Joseph Hensler Association, a fraternal group noted for its annual fun-filled shipboard outing to College Point, New York, and parades through the Ironbound neighborhood.

Hensler Brewery operations managed to keep afloat through the Prohibition years before shutting down for good in 1958.

'Pride of Newark'

Another German-born brewer, Christian Feigenspan, started making beer in a cellar in uptown Newark in 1875. Twelve years later he shifted operations Down Neck, where, at Freeman and Christie streets in the heart of the Twelfth Ward, the Christian Feigenspan Brewing Company would turn out countless barrels and bottles of lager for years to come.

An expansive brewery plant was built in 1891, its main office at 50 Freeman Street while Feigenspan resided at 18 Freeman. His death in 1899 brought son Christian to the firm's helm. In a city rife with breweries, the company's large "P.O.N." sign – for "Pride of Newark" – featuring an illuminated blob-top bottle, helped give Feigenspan top billing for years. The brightly-lit logo kept blazing away during Prohibition despite the plant being shut down. But the Feigenspan aura eventually faded when, fiscally weakened by the Depression, the company in 1943 was absorbed by Robert Ballantine, of P. Ballantine & Sons, and operated for a few more years.

Barons of Business

Business fortunes were made by other than brewers, too, in the eastern Newark territory that bustled with Industrial Age dynamism. The following are sketches of some of the more enterprising and notable among them:

In 1882, the inventor Edward Weston, maker of electrical instruments, established the Newark Electric Light and Power Company, on Mechanic Street (later renamed Edison Place), and developed street lighting.

Born in England, Weston settled in Newark in 1875 and perfected a process for zinc electroplating. His electric carbon arc-lamp illuminated factories, railways, and bridges, including the Brooklyn Bridge. The first public use of electric lamps in the United States was carried out to illuminate Military Park in Newark.

Silver and Gold

The German-born Edward Balbach settled in Newark in 1850 and, using gold and silver recovered from floor sweepings in the city's jewelry factories, revolutionized

CHRISTIAN FEIGENSPAN OPERATED ONE OF NEWARK'S LARGEST BREWERIES IN THE IRONBOUND DISTRICT FOR MORE THAN FOUR DECADES, STARTING IN THE LATE 1880S.

John Wesley Hyatt (top) and Franklin Murphy (bottom).

gold and silver refining in America to make his fortune. Edward Balbach & Son plants were situated on River Street (later, Raymond Boulevard), close by the Passaic River, and the Balbachs – Edward Sr. and Edward Jr. – became a combined powerhouse in social circles there, entertaining in grand style at their nearby residences.

One exemplary occasion took place in October, 1884, with a reception for Democratic presidential candidate Grover Cleveland. He rode in the younger Edward Balbach's carriage in a festive procession from the Market Street Station east on Market Street to Ferguson Street and thence to the Balbach Jr. mansion fronting on River Street – adjacent to the Morris Canal – the mansion gaily illuminated by Chinese lanterns and host to a crowd of dignitaries and citizens.

Two years later, when President Cleveland participated in dedication ceremonies for the newly installed Statue of Liberty in New York Harbor, the Balbachs hired an excursion steamer to take a boatload of friends and patrons down the Passaic River to the celebration. Part of the Balbach property on River Street later became the site of Riverbank Park, the public recreational area.

Bone Crushers

Drawing on the use of a bone-grinding machine he brought with him from his native England, the emigrant Joseph Lister in 1861 established the Passaic Carbon and Agricultural Chemical Works on land fronting on the Passaic River deep in the "Neck" area of eastern Newark. The company became a major supplier of sulphuric acid for oil refineries and other industrial concerns in North America.

Lister was succeeded by his sons Alfred and Edwin, and their success in manufacturing fertilizers for farmers from horse, cattle, and buffalo bones shipped from the American West brought them a fortune. Their "chemical works" business by the river, quickly growing to more than a dozen buildings, was most famously known as the Lister Brothers operation and, more infamously, as a predecessor of industrial activity spewing forth various forms of pollutants near the river – and directly in it. The enterprise founded by the brothers gave its name to Lister Avenue.

Alfred Lister committed suicide in 1890 by jumping from a steamship in the Caribbean Sea following a business deal that went sour. He had sold his stock in the family firm, then known as the Lister Agricultural Chemical Company, and invested in a new fertilizer company, in the process losing practically all of his fortune.

Varnish and Celluloid

In 1865, a precocious businessman named Franklin Murphy, a Civil War veteran still shy of his twentieth year, established a varnish-producing firm he named Murphy & Co. Starting with one factory at the intersection of McWhorter and Chestnut streets, it grew into the multi-building Murphy Varnish Company complex – enhancing Newark's growing reputation as America's varnish capital.

The half-dozen Murphy factories in the McWhorter-Chestnut area employed some two hundred workmen at its peak, and their founder made a name for himself in public affairs – member of the Newark Common Council, state assemblyman, state Republican chairman, Governor of New Jersey. Progressive in his political outlook, he pushed for the establishment of recreational outlets for young people – an effort fulfilled in the Ironbound with the creation of Riverbank Park adjacent to the Morris Canal-Passaic River area.

John Wesley Hyatt, who invented the first commercially successful synthetic plastic, relocated from Albany, New York, in 1872 to establish a Down Neck toehold with an enterprise that became the

THE LISTER AGRICULTURAL CHEMICAL WORKS PRODUCED FERTILIZER AND OTHER CHEMICALS FROM ANIMAL BONES SHIPPED FROM THE WEST.

Celluloid Corporation of America. In a new five-story factory on Mechanic Street (Edison Place), he produced his ivory-like plastic. "Celluloid" was used in the making of billiard balls, dentures, and other items subsequently at a large factory complex established farther east in Newark in an area bounded by Ferry, Magazine, Niagara, and Darcy streets, adjacent to what was still largely undeveloped farmland.

Over generations, the Celluloid office at 295 Ferry Street was home base for the company's managers and thousands of employees. Company operations in Newark were plagued over the years, however, by a fire hazard that attaches to the basic material of cellulose nitrate – by at least one count, thirty-nine fires occurred over a span of thirty-six years, exacting a toll of nine lives and many injuries.

Platinum and Iron

A onetime jewelry salesman named Charles W. Engelhard acquired a platinum company on New Jersey Railroad Avenue in a 1902 deal that would lead ultimately to establishment of the Engelhard Corporation.

A year after taking control of the Charles F. Croselmire Company, Engelhard created the American Platinum Works, on New Jersey Railroad Avenue (which, along with the railway itself, constitutes the Ironbound's western perimeter). Further acquisitions increased his holdings in an area extending from Oliver to Chestnut streets and beyond.

Engelhard, who emigrated from Germany in 1891, also created the Hanovia Chemical and Manufacturing Company in Newark and became the world's largest refiner and fabricator of platinum metals, gold, and silver. His son, Charles W. Engelhard Jr., would become known as the "Platinum King" whose persona was an inspiration for writer

BAKER & CO. PLATINUM REFINERS ON NEW JERSEY RAILROAD AVENUE.

Ian Fleming's notorious "Gold-finger" character of literary and cinematic expression.

Iron foundries were an Ironbound staple. One leading business in that realm was Maher & Flockhart, which began turning out iron products at Polk and Clover streets in 1889. The firm had been founded seven years earlier by the Irish-born Edward Maher and the Scottish-born James Flockhart.

The products were cast from molten iron issuing forth from furnaces, perhaps most recognizable among them – at least in the public mind – being sewer plates and manhole covers bearing the "Flockhart" stamp. After Maher's death in 1907, the firm became known as the Flockhart Foundry.

There were annual outings to places such as Paterson, arranged by the employee association known as the Maher & Flockhart Guards. Such days traditionally began with a parade that formed at the company complex on Polk Street with a complement of hundreds of members and guests. Accompanied by a musical band, it would proceed amid the shrill of factory whistles and the waving of banners to Ferry, Market, and Broad streets in downtown Newark. And then it was off to a day of fun and games.

In the Money

The imposing if slightly peculiar-looking building that became an Ironbound landmark, as well as the symbolic gateway to the neighborhood, opened for business on July 25, 1910. It was the Ironbound Trust Company, at Ferry and Market streets – surely seeking to capitalize on the growing residential, commercial, and industrial

Considering the quantity of beer produced in the "Ironbound District," the neighborhood might just as well have been named "Beer Island."
—Willard Price, 1918

activity taking place Down Neck.

The new bank had occupied quarters at 11 Ferry Street for three years until construction of a flatiron-type building of classic design was completed. It was designed by the architect John H. Ely – one of the Ironbound's more distinguished residents – and built at a cost of about $50,000. It featured a pair of white marble columns in front, pilasters flanking tall windows on each side, and an expansive skylight that illuminated the interior.

Sitting across from it was the Market Street Station and the (now elevated) Pennsylvania Railroad tracks. The property was formerly owned by William A. Righter, prominent Newark attorney, landowner, Civil War soldier, and civic leader.

A branch office of Ironbound Trust was established at a later date farther east at 210 Ferry Street. The company was the creation of a group of businessmen and Newark civic leaders, including City Controller J. Henry Bacheller and manufacturer Richard C. Jenkinson. Bacheller headed the bank from 1908 to 1927, at which point it was taken over by the Fidelity Union Trust Company. That larger Newark entity also, in 1930, acquired another Ironbound bank, the Equitable Trust Company.

The bank's opening probably signified more than anything else the growing frequency of usage of the "Ironbound" descriptive. By 1920, there were sixteen separate listings in the Newark city directory that employed the title, ranging alphabetically from the Ironbound Amusement Co. (operators of the Victor Theatre at 128 Wilson Avenue) to the Ironbound Trust Co.

Leather Goods

The growing market for cars as the twentieth century began to unfold helped to stimulate a demand for leather upholstery – good news for such Newark manufacturers as Blanchard Bro. & Lane, with offices at 20 Bruen Street in the Ironbound.

The city had long occupied a leading position in the nation's patent-leather industry, accounting in some years for as much as ninety per cent of its manufacture, and the Ironbound had its share of such firms. By about the year 1910, Blanchard Bro. & Lane employed some three hundred skilled workmen turning out, in addition to auto upholstery, enameled and fancy colored leather for carriages, shoes, furniture, and the saddlery trades at its block-long complex bounded by Bruen, Hamilton, and McWhorter streets.

The firm had been founded in 1860 by Noah F. Blanchard, who was joined in its management by brothers David, Samuel, and Charles, and a year later it took in P. Van Zandt Lane as a partner. Noah F. Blanchard, who died in 1881, had also been an early president of the Prudential Insurance Co.

There could be, however, bothersome aspects for those who lived near the incessant operations of large-scale industrial sites like the Blanchard enterprise, such as, for example, pervasive odors. Nonetheless, manufacturers frequently found their interests defended in the face of such criticism. An editorial in the *Newark Evening News* in 1898, for example, had extolled the supposedly beneficial qualities of the city's leather factories. "Odors of the tanyard are not only beneficial to the dwellers in the surrounding neighborhood, but are positively healthful and fattening," the editorial asserted. "Of course, it takes time for people to get acclimated, as it were …"

The Not-so-Sweet Smell of Success

There was also the hazard of such criminal behavior as payroll robberies. As happened, for example, on a Saturday in April of 1927 when, just before noon, four men brandishing shotguns and pistols stole the weekly cash payroll from office personnel at the Heller & Merz plant on Wilson Avenue. Jumping into a stolen black Cadillac driven by a fifth member of the gang, they were last seen speeding away on New York Avenue with their loot, totaling $6,000.

The Heller & Merz complex, dominated by a 350-foot-tall smokestack, was a familiar presence for baseball fans watching games in the adjacent ballfield – at first called Wiedenmayer Park, then Davids Stadium, followed by Bear Stadium and, finally, Ruppert Stadium. The noxious fumes emitted by the company in the course of its production of chemical dyes, compounded by the natural smells arising from the Newark meadows, created an often malodorous ambience.

The company was founded in 1869 by German emigrants Henry Merz and Frederick Heller (Heller came over in 1849, Merz in 1853). They started on River Street with two small furnaces before moving three years later to the larger property on Hamburg Place. The firm, a leader in the field of manufacturing aniline colors for dyeing purposes with cotton, wool, silk and leather, was bought out in 1930 by American Cyanamid.

We All Scream for …

In 1927, the Breyer Ice Cream Co., a division of the National Dairy Products Corporation, opened a plant on Passaic Avenue, between Chapel and Waydell streets, in the Twelfth Ward. The plant, an offshoot of a Philadelphia company that got its start in 1866, became a landmark thanks to its large roof-top sign. The sign flashed an illuminated "Breyer's" logo that could be seen from miles beyond.

Also notable were the ice-cream company's Dixie Cup lids which, when removed, displayed head-shot photos of the reigning movie stars of the day. The company got started soon after William Breyer hand-cranked his first gallon of ice cream in the kitchen of his Philadelphia home. Production at the Ironbound plant on Passaic Avenue (later, Raymond Boulevard) was discontinued in 1968 by the Breyer's parent company Kraftco and shifted to Long Island, New York.

Be It Ever So Humble

Workers needed a place to live, the cheaper the better. On November 12, 1930, ground was broken for

Newark's first low-income housing project, to become widely known as the "Prudential Apartments," on land in the Ironbound's Twelfth Ward that was owned by the Prudential Insurance Company.

Billed as a "model tenement house development," the complex went up on a portion of property on Raymond Boulevard. There were six buildings in all, with courtyards. The property stretched a city block in length between Lexington and Oxford streets and extended to Fleming Avenue. The complex was completed in 1932 and formally named for a Prudential director, Chellis Austin, who died as the development was taking shape.

The apartments housed four hundred and seven families. The project, in which the City of Newark was a participant, was billed as an experiment in providing "medium-cost housing" for people of lesser incomes – the monthly rent could be as little as thirty-six dollars. Prudential sold the complex in 1952. Similar complexes built in the Ironbound were Pennington Court (1939, named for a former New Jersey governor) at South and Pacific streets in the Tenth Ward, and Hyatt Court (1942, named for Celluloid founder John Wesley Hyatt) in the Hawkins Street area of the Twelfth Ward.

FEMALE WORKERS IN 1916 DURING A RECREATION PERIOD AT THE HYATT ROLLER BEARING COMPANY, FOUNDED BY NEWARK INVENTOR AND INDUSTRIALIST JOHN WESLEY HYATT IN 1892.

THE PUBLIC GOOD

The big news at the time was the discovery of gold in them thar hills of California. But for a group of workmen in Newark, their focus in 1849 was on building a public school on Lafayette Street that would be the first one east of the railroad tracks.

The school had been authorized by the Newark Common Council the previous July in accordance with the terms of the municipal Charter of 1836 stipulating, in effect, that each of the city's four wards have public schools. And so, with construction complete, doors were opened for the first time to prospective students on July 27, 1849, at the Fifth Ward Grammar School. The tract accommodating the school, which cost four thousand and five hundred dollars to build, fronted on Lafayette Street and extended from Prospect to Congress streets.

In the mid-1870s, the Fifth Ward Grammar School was renamed Lafayette Street School. It survives today as the most venerable of its kind in Newark, one of the oldest public schools in New Jersey.

Texas Hoodlums

The brothers Joseph and Samuel Clark were teachers and administrators at Lafayette for a good part of the second half of the century, Joseph as principal from 1857 to 1894, while Samuel headed the Evening School for Males there starting in 1849. The latter's duties at the outset included supervision of a couple of hundred neighborhood youths, a number of whom achieved notoriety as the "Rock Boys." They were described as such in an 1893 publication as "a gang of hoodlums that terrorized that portion of the city," without further elaboration. We are left to wonder whether the description perhaps reflected a degree of social instability that might be found in a fast-growing locale sometimes known then as "Texas," as a Newark old-timer remembered the neighborhood many years later.

The school on Lafayette Street must have been relatively tiny at first. It was enlarged in 1863, and another floor was added in 1870. Further additions were made in 1881, 1884, and 1904. Grandest of all was a rebuilding project carried out in 1909 that provided fifteen more classrooms as well as an auditorium with seven hundred seats, a gymnasium, separate toilets for boys and girls, a kind of English garden forecourt (the renovation added a Tudor design to the school's appearance), and a roof capable of use for both dance and calisthenics.

Another school was added in 1857, this one for

the newly created Twelfth Ward. Opened on May 4, a Monday, it was initially designated as Public School No. 9 and also known as the Twelfth Ward Public School before becoming, finally, the South Market Street School. Its address was 699 Market, near Mott Street.

The first principal was Samuel W. Clark, the teacher-administrator regularly assigned to the Fifth Ward Public School on Lafayette Street. A kindergarten was added at South Market Street School in 1893, and the building was enlarged in 1899. A *Newark Evening News* writer in October 1911 opined that the school "should be abandoned" owing to its location in a "noisy" area, the din of street traffic, and its close proximity to a Central Railroad of New Jersey freight terminal. In later years it was, in fact, phased out of existence.

Finally, children living in the Tenth Ward got their own school there as of September 6, 1869, this one on Oliver Street. It operated as the Tenth Ward Grammar School for a number of years until its eventually permanent redesignation as Oliver Street School.

Lots of Students

Newark was undergoing much growth, in population and building activity, in the latter part of the nineteenth century and the early years of the twentieth, growth that included school construction. Between the years 1880 and 1917, for example, a total of forty-four schools went up in Newark, and there were as well seventy-six additions tacked on.

Population growth, much of it German in origin, was occurring in the Twelfth Ward, where, on April 10, 1882, doors opened to pupils for the first time at Hamburg Place School – later to become the Wilson Avenue School. The small red-brick building was at 25 Hamburg Place, near Ferry Street. Its first principal, serving until 1897, was Frederick W. Fort, a nephew of former New Jersey Governor George F. Fort (1851-54).

In the mid-1870s, the Fifth Ward Grammar School was renamed Lafayette Street School. It survives today as the most venerable of its kind in Newark, one of the oldest public schools in New Jersey.

Hamburg Place School was merged with a larger adjacent building erected on the property and opened for classes on January 3, 1889. One of the school's first pupils was a future Mayor of Newark, Frederick Breidenbach. Enrollment at Hamburg Place climbed from four hundred in 1882 to about one thousand and six hundred in 1895, making it one of Newark's largest in terms of numbers.

The building in 1907 got a ten-room addition that included a gymnasium, first of its kind in the city's school system. Also operating here for a brief period was the Hamburg Place Evening High School, one of four such night schools in Newark in the early years of the twentieth century.

Also opened on that same January 3, 1889, in the same Twelfth Ward, was the Hawkins Street School. Others erected in the nineteenth century were those on Walnut Street (1863), South Street (1884), and Ann Street (1892), in addition to facilities on Houston, Thomas, Clover, and Wall streets. All but Lafayette were in the Tenth and Twelfth wards, but not all survived.

It was a continued rise in enrollment at Hamburg Place School that prompted the need for another grade school in the vicinity, a need that was met by the construction of Ann Street School, between New York Avenue and Elm Road. Opened on September 12, 1892, and initially limited in size to a few classrooms, it was gradually enlarged. Frederick W. Fort, principal of Hamburg Place School, also headed Ann Street School for the first two years. It was effectively the last of the elementary schools to be erected on Newark's east side.

Higher Education

In his year-opening message to the public in January of 1904, Mayor Henry M. Doremus said that a second Newark high school was "sorely needed" – he pinpointed the city's southeast section as the desired locale. Also needed, Doremus said, was a commercial school offering a "first class business education."

Asserting that Newark High School was filled to capacity, the Mayor recommended "most strongly" that provision be made for a secondary school devoted to instruction in such practical skills as stenography, typewriting, and bookkeeping, through which "apt pupils could be immediately graduated into business houses where their future welfare would be assured."

Two years later, in 1906, the Board of Education took the necessary action that authorized creation of a high school on Newark's east side. The Board's members approved a purchase price of $42,600 for thirty lots in a block-long Ironbound tract as the site for an East Side Commercial and Manual Training

High School. It would be the second of its kind, after Newark High School, and the first to be shaped as much out of "practical" motivation as of a purely "literary" or liberal-arts bent.

Construction got under way, finally, in 1910. The site chosen was encompassed by Van Buren, Warwick, Nichols, and Tyler streets, with the proposed school to front on East Side Park (Tyler would later become Pulaski Street). While awaiting the completion of construction, first-year students received instruction at the Market Street School across from the Essex County Court House in central Newark.

The first day of April, 1911, was an important moment in Ironbound institutional history. Toting books and baggage, students and faculty on that Saturday moved into East Side High School – formally, East Side Commercial and Manual Training High School. That moving day marked the fulfillment

EAST SIDE COMMERCIAL AND MANUAL TRAINING HIGH SCHOOL OPENED TO STUDENTS IN 1911.

of years of hope and planning. Enrollment initially was two hundred and fifty, the principal was Thomas F. Kennedy, formerly of Barringer High School, and a sealed box of mementos was ceremonially buried under the flagpole out front.

After years of debate often focused on whether a "literary high school" would be fiscally prudent for an essentially blue-collar Down Neck neighborhood – a *Newark Evening News* editorialist, for one, thought not – three basic courses of study were offered: General, Commercial, and Technical. The General course, which included algebra and history in addition to electives in Latin and German, focused on academic preparation ("college prep") for university study and for "normal" (teacher training) schools, and thereby represented a victory for those arguing against an educational palette limited to "industrial and vocational studies" for Down Neck youth.

Fun and Games

Mayor Doremus also would complain, two years later, about a dearth of recreational space for youngsters residing on Newark's east side – specifically, the Twelfth Ward.

"The crowded conditions and the constantly increasing number of tenements in certain sections of the city renders it advisable for us to devise ways and means for the protection of children who are now growing up in the streets, the gutters and sidewalks of the Twelfth Ward," he asserted on January 5, 1906, in his traditional year-opening message delivered to the Newark Common Council. The remedy, Doremus said, was "a public park and breathing space where they may roam at will."

Recreational history directly involving the Down Neck neighborhood had already been made in 1895. It was then, on February 10, that the newly established Essex County Park Commission – first of its kind in the nation – approved the purchase and stitching together of thirteen pieces of land at the Ironbound's center, thereby giving the thickly congealing neighborhood a breath of fresh air through creation of an East Side Park.

That action proved to be a recreational and environmental uplift. The tract of nearly thirteen acres was bounded by Adams, Oliver, Walnut, and Van Buren streets, in the Tenth Ward. The county commission had been created to build neighborhood parks in densely settled areas. East Side Park, designed by the Olmsted Brothers of New York's Central Park fame, featured winding walkways and tree-lined promenades and was to prove a valued addition – even if sometimes tagged by locals as a bug-happy "Mosquito Park."

In 1906, acting on the recommendation of Mayor Doremus, a commission declared that, "after having carefully studied the needs of the people below the railroad," it found "that what they need and demand is a large recreation place … What they do not want is a large ornamental park surrounded with fences and restricting regulations." The end result, though still years away, would be the establishment of Riverbank Park along a stretch of the Passaic River.

MAYOR HENRY M. DOREMUS ADVOCATED FOR THE CONSTRUCTION OF A HIGH SCHOOL AND RECREATIONAL SPACE IN THE CROWDED PRECINCTS OF THE IRONBOUND DISTRICT.

Land was acquired and playground installation was begun in 1907, with a number of public figures with Ironbound connections being prominent in a campaign to establish such a park. They included Franklin Murphy, the Newark paint manufacturer and former Governor of New Jersey (1902-04), and the Reverend Michael A. McManus, pastor of nearby St. Aloysius Church, as well as Democratic "boss" William Harrigan.

Finally, in July of 1911, amid an industrial wasteland hard by the polluted Passaic River and an obsolete Morris Canal, the much-needed oasis of recreational greenery was officially opened to the public. Small in size – less than eleven acres

– Riverbank Park was endowed at first with only minimal playground equipment.

Also designed by the Olmsted Brothers firm, Riverbank Park had been brought into being by the Essex County Park Commission, utilizing property formerly owned by the Balbach Smelting and Refining Company. It would be the smallest in the county park system, a tract of land bounded by Market, Frederick, and Van Buren streets, and Passaic Avenue. (Frederick Street later became Somme Street, while Passaic Avenue would be renamed Raymond Boulevard.)

A section of the park, situated partially in the Fifth Ward and partially in the Twelfth Ward, included land once traversed by the Morris Canal. In the 1920s the park was expanded to include a grandstand and a sheltered area near the playground.

Learning to Swim ...

Another recreational outlet of a public nature became available for Ironbound residents in 1930. This was Hayes Park East, featuring a good-sized swimming pool and designed primarily for use by the offspring of working families in that part of Newark – especially welcome as the Great Depression wrought economic hardship for legions of financially strapped residents.

Ceremonies marking the official opening of Hayes Park East were held there on September 2. The park sported a flag provided by the Ironbound Manufacturers Association, and Mayor Jerome T. Congleton was among the ceremonial participants.

Named for Alice W. Hayes, a descendant of Newark founder Robert Treat, the park was situated on land that was part of the so-called "Island" district in a heavily industrial area of the Twelfth Ward – the district was bounded by Raymond Boulevard, Chapel Street, Lister Avenue, and Lockwood Street, and derived its "Island" name from the fact of its being separated by the Morris Canal from its geographic surroundings.

A couple of generations of Ironbound youngsters would frolic and learn to swim at little cost in the large pool at Hayes Park East. Miss Hayes's vast estate – she had died in 1914 – included nearly $1 million for the creation of parks in the city of which she was a lifelong resident. For the Hayes Park East property (ultimately at 608-630 Ferry Street), the city drew on the funds to acquire, through condemnation proceedings, a vacant tract of land measuring six hundred by four hundred feet owned by the estate of Frederick Bonykamper, a German-born Newark resident who was a city Alderman, representing the Twelfth Ward, in 1872. Neighborhood children had long helped themselves to utilizing the vacant lot as an unofficial playground.

… And to Read

Ironbound people also got their own full-fledged library center in 1923 – although, a bit peculiarly, the "Ironbound" descriptive was missing from its title. On Sunday, September 23, the Newark Free Public Library opened what was designated as its Van Buren Branch. Housed in a two-story building at 140 Van Buren Street, it and another (Springfield) branch were the first of several to be opened over the years to come, fulfilling the democratic-populist aspirations of the Library's distinguished director, John Cotton Dana.

Soon after coming to Newark in 1902, Dana was envisioning the opening of branches in rented space, usually in stores, around the city. By 1914, several years after the opening of a Ferry Street Branch in what Dana himself later conceded were "very inadequate quarters" at 205 Ferry, some four thousand volumes were made available for prospective borrowers, and "an increase in patronage" was manifested.

Regularly included in future holdings at the Van Buren Branch, situated amid a heavily immigrant locale, would be works in languages other than English. One of those long associated with the Library was Charles A. Baretski, an Ironbound product – raised on Pulaski Street – who became branch manager in 1954.

The Portuguese Presence

Recreational needs and social uplift also could be provided by the constituent parts – the various "nationalities" – within the larger Ironbound community, of which there were many (a total of fifty-four has been suggested). One example from a somewhat later period was the community that grew out of an original trickle of newcomers of Portuguese origin. A group of about thirty such people, meeting on December 17, 1921, formed a social-fraternal organization they called the Sport Clube Português – the Portuguese Sport Club.

The SCP, as it was often labeled, was the first of more than a score of such groups of that nationality to be established. It was, at least at first, a mostly male organization that initially occupied space at 13 Ferry Street (the future site, coincidentally, of Peter Francisco Park, memorializing a Revolutionary War hero reputed

NEWARK BALLPLAYERS JOE MCGINNITY (LEFT) AND LARRY
SCHLAFLY (RIGHT) PICTURED IN AMERICAN TOBACCO
COMPANY BASEBALL CARDS, *CIRCA* 1909.

to have been of Azorean origin), and then at 36 Downing
Street. Property at 51-55 Prospect Street then became
the site for construction of a spacious center, dedicated
on December 14, 1941.

The SCP would provide a venue for music,
theater, sporting events, and social activities, as well as
a school offering Portuguese-language classes designed
primarily for members' children. The Portuguese
presence in the Ironbound dates to the World War I
period, most of its people coming from the continent
in contradistinction to the traditional Azores-New
England connection that previously accounted for the
bulk of resettlement in the United States by members
of that nationality. One town in northern Portugal
particularly well represented was Murtosa, as signified
by the establishment in 1926 of another of the social
clubs, the Sport Maritimo Murtoense.

Baseball in the Meadowlands

Down Neck started as a venue for organized baseball competition going back to the 1890s and property owned by the Wiedenmayer family, of brewery renown. That tract was on land that sat near the eastern end of Hamburg Place in the Newark meadows. Thus began a succession of fields – Wiedenmayer Park, Davids Stadium (1926-31), Bear Stadium (1932-33), and Ruppert Stadium (1934-67).

There were many special moments, as for example in 1904 when fans in the Newark area got a rare chance to see some of the game's top major-leaguers, including Wee Willie Keeler, Sam Crawford, and Clark Griffith, as a glitch in their schedule caused the New York Highlanders (predecessor to the Yankees) to take on the Detroit Tigers in a Sunday game at Wiedenmayer Park. A crowd of more than six thousand turned out on that July day to see the Highlanders win 3-1 via pitcher-manager Griffith's meager allowance of only three hits.

There was also the Sunday double-header on September 12, 1909, that attracted a near-capacity crowd to Wiedenmayer Park to cheer pitcher-owner Joe "Iron Man" McGinnity as he hurled a three-hit shutout for the Newark Sailors against the Jersey City Skeeters in the second game after already having pitched in the opener.

In 1925, Newark lost its baseball standard-bearer when the Bears, with a less than perfect 8-20 record, left the city for Providence, Rhode Island, following a fire that wrecked Wiedenmayer Park. A new owner, Charles A. Davids, acquired a Pennsylvania franchise and transferred it to Newark, and a new ballpark of steel and concrete was built on a fifteen-acre plot of land, adjacent to the site of the original field, bounded by Wilson Avenue and Avenues K and L.

That venue, especially in its most celebrated phase as Ruppert Stadium, went on to accommodate paying crowds of as many as fifteen thousand patrons as host for four decades to the Newark Bears of the International League, and a farm club and talent pool for the mighty New York Yankees baseball empire.

OH, HAPPY DAY

A mood of expectation pervaded Penn Station on October 7, 1937, as baseball fans impatiently awaited the arrival of a train carrying their triumphant Newark Bears after a sensational championship season. Then, with a cadre of police guarding against any display of over-the-top exuberance, the Bears disembarked from their Pullman car as a brass band belted out "Happy Days Are Here Again." The ballplayers filed out to Raymond Plaza and the waiting cars that would convey them to Broad Street and a downtown mini-parade.

Loaded with talent – big bats Charlie Keller and Joe Gordon, ace pitchers like Spud Chandler and Atley Donald – the Bears reigned supreme all season long, writing a bright chapter in the mostly glorious saga that began when "Colonel" Jacob Ruppert, a beer baron with deep pockets, bought the team in 1931 and made it a New York Yankees subsidiary. In the process, the ballpark on Wilson Avenue amid the Newark meadows – once the site of Wiedenmayer Park and then of Davids Stadium – became Ruppert Stadium.

And what especially delighted their fans in copping the Little World Series title that glorious week in 1937 is the way they did it. After somehow managing to drop three games in a row at their Ruppert Stadium digs down in the Ironbound, they proceeded to vanquish the Columbus Redbirds in four straight contests – out in Ohio!

In baseball annals, it was one for the books – although effectively replicated nine years later when the home-team Newark Eagles came from behind to top the Kansas City Monarchs in the 1946 Negro League World Series. It was a kind of last hurrah for pro ball Down Neck – Ruppert Stadium was soon phased out, destined for demolition in 1967.

⫶ A WORSHIPFUL PLACE ⫶

In addition to its reputation as a manufacturers' haven and an opportune workplace for laborers, Down Neck has traditionally been associated with a quite different trait – being regarded as a religious-minded place replete with houses of worship, a so-called "community of churches." The fact is, of course, that churchgoers at a very early period in that neck of the wood would have had to travel elsewhere for any kind of spiritual nourishment, there being, in religious terms, no there there. Until, at any event, Methodists of characteristically evangelical-minded bent broke the ice by establishing a mission on Union Street.

There had been efforts to reach mariners and boatmen who frequented the city's bustling docks – a Bethel Mission appears to have been operating at least as early as 1840 on South Market Street east of the New Jersey Railroad line at the Passaic River. But not until January 6, 1847, was the first permanent church organized. This was the Union Street Missionary Church, representing an outreach by the Franklin Street Methodist Episcopal Church, of central Newark, that was designed to establish a Sunday school for youngsters living on the other side of the tracks.

This was the beginning of the Union Street Methodist Church. The first congregational meetings were held in a carpenter shop on Prospect Street, followed by erection of a wooden house of worship in 1849, soon to be replaced by a more substantial brick structure at 143 Union, at the corner of Green Street, that was dedicated in May of 1850. The first pastor was the Reverend J. P. Fort. (The church's initial address, briefly, was 125 Union.)

It was also a missionary effort that brought about the establishment of a Dutch Reformed parish east of the New Jersey Railroad tracks. The Second Reformed Church was organized on May 23, 1848, by worshippers at the First Reformed Church in central Newark. Initial meetings were held in a small chapel on McWhorter Street, near Ferry, before construction of a brick edifice with a 120-foot spire at that intersection.

The church was designed by William H. Kirk, a builder-architect and First Reformed member who

LEFT: St. James Roman Catholic Church at Lafayette and Jefferson streets, about 1870.

was a vital force in establishing the new congregation. Dedication ceremonies were held on May 8, 1849. One of the more renowned pastors in the church's history was the Reverend Gustavus Abeel (1849-64), of old New York Dutch family origins. Four decades after its founding the congregation would move on, relocating in 1888 from Ferry and McWhorter, a location in the Fifth Ward that was already becoming hemmed in by commercial activity, to a less bustling and more residential address on New York Avenue at Pacific Street in the Tenth Ward.

In the process, it also underwent a change of name, now calling itself the New York Avenue Reformed Church. The congregation at first worshipped in a chapel before erecting a fully suitable church at New York Avenue and Pacific Street. A cornerstone was laid in October of 1891, and construction was completed by the following December. The congregation managed to pay off its heavy indebtedness by Christmas Day in 1895. The Reverend John S. Allen headed the church until 1906, overseeing such building improvements as the construction of an addition for Sunday-school instruction and the installation of a pipe organ. This was, as he once told a *Newark Evening News* reporter,

a time of extreme makeover in a changing urban environment. "Members move away as fast as they come in, and there is a constant change."

Eventually, in 1940, the congregation's shrinking numbers led to the New York Reformed parish merging with the Third Reformed Church – also known as North Reformed – located on Broad Street in Newark. (The old building at Ferry and McWhorter streets that accommodated the original Second Reformed congregation had long since been passed on for a new identity as Our Lady of Mount Carmel Church – itself eventually relocating many years later to greener pastures on Oliver Street, also in the Tenth Ward.)

Trinity Reformed

Newark's east side became the locale of another Dutch Reformed congregation in 1869. Designated at first as East Reformed and also known as the East Church, it later became – as of December 20, 1894 – Trinity Reformed Church. It made its home at 479 Ferry Street, at Hawkins Street, in the city's easternmost area.

The first pastor was the Reverend Isaac P. Brokaw, who served from 1869 to 1874. He had been instrumental in organizing the church, along with thirty-four communicants, although the congregation actually had roots that dated as far back as about 1850. Services had been held originally, starting in 1867, in a chapel near Ferry and Bowery (Bowery Street would later become Fleming Avenue), an area that was as yet only sparsely settled. The chapel had actually been replanted there after several years' use by the Second Reformed Church, at the other end of Ferry Street, as a mission effort.

In 1870, a new edifice was erected, and in 1908 the entire Trinity Reformed Church property was rededicated after a renovation.

Stansbury's Church

The first rector of what became Christ Episcopal Church was the Reverend Robert T. S. Lowell, of Boston Brahmin lineage – he was an older brother of the eminent poet-author James Russell Lowell. It was on February 2, 1850, that the Christ Free

Mission Church – famously open to all regardless of financial means – was consecrated at 76 Prospect Street by the Episcopal bishop of New Jersey, George Washington Doane.

Robert Trail Spencer Lowell was a driving force behind what became Christ Episcopal Church, long an entity on this Down Neck property extending from Prospect to Congress streets. Initial meetings were held as early as 1848 in a room at the corner of Union and Lafayette streets, and the perceived need for a larger sanctuary brought about construction of a brownstone edifice designed by Gothic-revival stylist Frank Willis.

In gratitude for his service, Christ Church parishioners in 1859 gave Reverend Lowell a two-volume collection of poet-author George Herbert's works. In a much later era, that two-volume set would figure at one point in the famous correspondence that ensued between poets Robert Lowell and Elizabeth Bishop – he had given the books as a going-away gift to Bishop, bound for Brazil and her long notable residence there.

More famous even than Reverend Lowell, in the history at least of this little old Down Neck institution that was Christ Episcopal Church, was his successor, J. Nicholas Stansbury. An important presence in Christian and charitable activities in the Newark region for decades, Dean Stansbury had a long (1859-91) stewardship at what became known as "Stansbury's Church." (Its site is on property that today accommodates the Roman Catholic sanctuary of Our Lady of Fatima Church.)

Fifth Baptist

In April of 1853 or thereabouts, the Reverend Thomas G. Wright began preaching on Sunday afternoons at places in the Fifth Ward. From this effort, fostered by the Newark Baptist City Mission, would arise the parish that became the Fifth Baptist Church, long a presence at the corner of Lafayette and Prospect streets.

Known at first as the Fifth Ward Mission and also as the Fourth Baptist Church, its initial meetings were held at Humanity Hall, 101 Union Street, with

FIFTH BAPTIST CHURCH WAS ERECTED IN 1855 AT LAFAYETTE AND PROSPECT STREETS. THE BUILDING WAS OCCUPIED BY A ROMAN CATHOLIC CONGREGATION IN 1928 AND RENAMED ST. JOSEPH'S CHURCH.

again in 1896. It would be transformed in 1928 into a Roman Catholic sanctuary, St. Joseph's Church, primarily for Spanish and Portuguese worshippers. St. Joseph's was organized by a Spanish order of Franciscan priests and represented families of both those nationalities (increasing numbers of Galicians had been settling in the Ironbound, as well as Portuguese, since the World War I period).

St. Joseph's became notable for its catacombs, installed in the church basement, displaying wax replicas of such martyred saints as Cecilia, Filomena, Ines, and Genaro. The first pastor of St. Joseph's was the Reverend Anthony Frontera, followed by the Reverend Michael Vidal, both of them Spanish-born.

German Congregations

Two congregations for German Protestants on Newark's east side were established in 1863 as the Civil War pitting North against South raged on. One of them was the Third German Presbyterian Church, in the Fifth Ward. It held its first services on March 30 at 85 Madison Street at the intersection with Ferry Street. The Reverend G. C. Seibert was pastor until 1872 (he was later on the faculty of the German Theological Seminary in Bloomfield). His successor was the Reverend Oscar Kraft, a Lutheran who in 1874 did much to cause three-fourths of church members to leave the Presbyterian fold. They thereupon formed the foundation of St. Stephan's German Evangelical and Lutheran Church.

the Reverend C. W. Waterhouse presiding. In March, 1855, the Reverend David T. Morrill became its first pastor, and a church building in Greek-revival style was erected on the Lafayette-Prospect property, land that was owned by Horace M. Baldwin. The new structure was dedicated on April 21, 1858.

The church officially became Fifth Baptist in 1869, a year that also marked the beginning of the pastorate of the Reverend David C. Hughes. His son, Charles Evans Hughes, would become a Republican candidate for President of the United States in 1916, nearly defeating the incumbent, Woodrow Wilson. Fifth Baptist Church underwent remodeling in 1872 and

The new minister at Third German Presbyterian, installed on June 9, 1875, was the Reverend Julius H. Wolff. In 1882 his church relocated to Hamburg Place, at Ann Street, where it became a neighborhood fixture, only a few city blocks distant from St. Stephan's, of even more landmark prominence.

Also established in 1863, in June, was a congregation for German Baptists. Organized as the Twelfth Ward Mission Chapel, it also became known as the Second German Baptist Church. A chapel was erected at Niagara and Paterson streets, at a cost of about $5,000, to be dedicated on Sunday, September 4. The Reverend J. C. Kraft headed the church from 1866 to 1879. The congregation later relocated to 367 Walnut Street, between Van Buren and Pulaski streets, and became frequently referred to as the Walnut Street Baptist Church.

An Ironbound Landmark

In 1874, the church that became an icon as a Down Neck landmark was established. It was, and remains, poised prominently as a kind of guardian over the so-called "Five Corners" intersection of Ferry Street and Hamburg Place – the future Wilson Avenue. It is St. Stephan's German and Evangelical Reformed Church.

It was founded by worshippers who broke away in a mass exodus from Third Presbyterian Church as a result of meetings that started taking place around 1872 in carpenter J. D. Reichart's property on Van Buren Street. The initial congregational service was held on March 22, 1874, under the first pastor, the Reverend Oscar Kraft.

The church building ensconced at the busy intersection, occupying a prominent place in a largely German area, was completed by December of 1874. Designed by George Staehlin, it is marked by a red-brick exterior done in Romanesque style with a white tower and a cornerstone a cornerstone with the following inscription: Erbaut A.D. 1874.

The interior featured imported German woodcarving with a carousel, among other features, many of the decorations being donations of the Hensler brewery family. Most notable of the church's

pastors over the years were Richard Katerndahl and Edward Fuhrmann, as well as the latter's son F. G. Walter Fuhrmann.

Long a United Church of Christ affiliate in later years, it eventually morphed into St. Stephan's Grace Community Church, becoming host to Spanish- and Portuguese-speaking Lutheran worshippers. The church appeared as a backdrop to action in the 2005 Stephen Spielberg-Tom Cruise film spectacle *War of the Worlds*.

Wild Things

A visit to the Ironbound in November of 1911 by a young Christian evangelist from New York City, seeking prospects among the area's growing Italian immigrant population, did much to establish a Presbyterian parish locally for worshippers of that nationality. This was the East Side Italian Church, at 240 Pacific Street.

"The result was that we rented the first floor of a house for thirteen dollars a month and began on Saturday with a sewing school of thirty-five little Italians (wild Indians!)," the Reverend Davis W. Lusk recalled in an article he authored in 1918 for the *Home Mission Monthly*. The article was entitled "The New American City: Fifty-Four Nationalities." Lusk, a onetime Ironbound minister who became superintendent of missions for the Presbytery of Newark, noted in his article that, as the Puritan settlers pushed aside Indian inhabitants, "now the descendants of these Puritans are being driven out by people from Southern Europe."

Leading the newly established parish, affiliated with the First Italian Presbyterian Church of central Newark, was the Reverend Peter Di Nardo. Preaching was done in a large hall, open-air meetings were held in summertime, and a Sunday school was established, along with a Christian Endeavor Society and groups for Boy Scouts and Camp Fire Girls.

Population Shift

Perhaps most symbolic of the demographic makeover that affected Protestant Christians on Newark's east side is the history of the venerable Sixth Presbyterian Church. It is a history that goes back to November

24, 1847, when thirty-seven members of Presbyterian churches and groups in Newark gathered at an address on Union Street to plant the seeds for what became the Sixth Presbyterian Church. Its formal organization came on October 1, 1848.

The church started life with about 250 members, including a seven-man board of overseers that included Horace J. Poinier, a lumber merchant – he resided at 50 Ferry Street and did business on Commercial Street close to the railway and the Passaic River – and a future Mayor of Newark. A church building was erected at 88 Union Street, facing Hamilton Street, that was dedicated in December, 1849.

The first pastor was a young Reverend William Aikman, just twenty-five years of age. A full six decades later, in October of 1908, Dr. Aikman would return to

An Ironbound landmark, St. Stephan's Church has stood at the "Five Corners" since 1874.

a much changed Newark for an anniversary celebration at which he evoked olden times in this neighborhood now coming to be known as "the Ironbound."

"The edifice which was then the home of the Sixth Church was not quite furnished, but being all young we were able to grow as we went along," he told the latter-day congregants, recalling – as reported in the *Newark Evening News* – an incipient place of worship. "Our church was then on Commerce Street … the little congregation and its little building. I have a lantern at home that was given to me when I was pastor here. This same lantern was used to show my wife and me the way across the lots and swamps which we had to traverse to get to the church … I am amazed at the city that has grown up where open fields were when I was in this place."

The Sixth Presbyterian congregation had moved on, in November of 1891, to a larger sanctuary on Lafayette Street, near Union. Its handsome new church there was a brownstone structure, Romanesque in style, designed by the Newark-born architect William Halsey Wood. And its pastor since 1885 was the Reverend Davis W. Lusk, who in 1910, on his own anniversary of service, recalled that when he started "our people lived in the immediate neighborhood, now they come from all parts of the city, even the suburban districts."

Lusk noted, as reported in the *News*, that he was the only pastor still around in 1910 from twenty-five years earlier except for "who was here when I came, and that is my neighbor, Father Cody of St. James's Catholic Church." Reverend Lusk ended his Sixth Presbyterian pastorate on April 12, 1911, having preached more than 2,000 sermons, performed 350 marriages, presided at 500 baptisms, and conducted 600 funerals during his Down Neck tenure.

The property at 88 Union Street that was formerly occupied by the Sixth Presbyterian Church was acquired around 1906 by the trustees of St. James African Methodist Episcopal Church. The Reverend H.P. Anderson was pastor. St. James remained on Union Street until 1945, when the congregation moved uptown to an imposing structure on Newark's High Street (predecessor to Martin Luther King Boulevard).

REV. DAVIS W. LUSK, PASTOR OF SIXTH PRESBYTERIAN CHURCH FROM 1885 TO 1911.

The origins of St. James AME date as far back as 1842, when its forerunner congregation was organized as Bethel AME Church, on Green Street. The labor needs of railroad contractors were a spur to increased settlement by African-Americans in the region, including areas of the Ironbound. "Men of all nationalities engaged in the building of the tunnels, Negroes doing the major part of the work," the *New York Times* reported on April 3, 1910, in a front-page article.

In 1931, another African-American congregation, St. Mark's Union AME Church, took over another venerable sanctuary, the Union Street Methodist Church at 141 Union, oldest of all churches in the Ironbound. In 1944, St. Mark's became Providence Baptist Church.

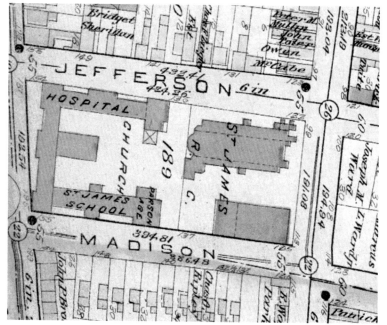

The Winds of Change

On a Sunday in September of 1928, a year away from the economic crash that would bring irreparable change to the American socio-political dynamic, the pastor of one of the Ironbound's oldest congregations called for the community's Protestants to band together.

The speaker was the Reverend Charles F. Bazata, pastor of Sixth Presbyterian Church, preaching a sermon on September 23 on an occasion that marked his twelfth anniversary as pastor of the church on Lafayette Street. Bazata, as the *Newark Evening News* reported, expressed the belief "that it has become absolutely necessary to weld together what is left of the Protestant forces in this sector into two or three strong churches adequately equipped, strongly financed and efficiently staffed …"

"If that is not done, Protestantism will fade out of the picture here completely and it will lose one of the finest opportunities for doing a much-needed work in one of the most strategic spots in one of the greatest industrial centers in the world."

Bazata, himself the son of immigrants from Bohemia, said changes in the neighborhood's sociological makeup were marked as early as the turn of the century, escalating thereafter until "the foreign invasion began in dead earnest. Lithuanians, Poles, Italians and others poured into the Ironbound section by the thousands. Then, in real earnest began the American exodus. As fast as the Slavs and Latins came in, the Americans went out …"

A Portuguese Congregation

Less than two years later, in June of 1930, a religious service was held for the first time for a small group of Portuguese-born Presbyterians at the Sixth Presbyterian Church, on Lafayette Street. The service represented the first fruits of an organizing effort that had begun the previous year, the congregants being guided by the Reverend Samuel S. Rizzo.

Rizzo was a young Brazilian minister who was studying at Columbia University in New York City for a doctorate. He had now accepted an invitation from the Newark Presbytery to ally himself with the incipient congregation. And in 1931 it took over a vacant building at Lafayette and Pulaski streets that was formerly owned by the Presbyterian Tabernacle Church. The new congregation, on October 13, 1935, was officially constituted as The Portuguese Evangelical Church.

In 1937, when Sixth Presbyterian's greatly reduced congregation caused it to lessen its role to one of mission status, the church sanctuary at Lafayette and Union was taken over by the Portuguese Presbyterians, with the permission of the Newark Presbytery. Congregants adopted the name St. Paul's United Presbyterian Church before changing it to St. Paul's Presbyterian Church – in Portuguese, the Igreja Presbiteriana São Paulo.

Reverend Rizzo was pastor until December 21, 1945, after which he left for Portugal to undertake missionary work there. He was succeeded by the Reverend Anthony A. Monteiro, whose pastorate at St. Paul's lasted until his death in 1974.

St. James Standing Tall

The cornerstone for what would become the Ironbound's grandest house of worship – and its first Roman Catholic presence – was installed on a Sunday in June of 1854 by Bishop James Roosevelt Bayley, first shepherd of the Diocese of Newark and an organizer of the institution that became Seton Hall University. This was St. James Church, long to become a landmark at Lafayette and Madison streets (over the years the apostrophe in the original St. James' title would be gradually subsumed as dispensable).

The Roman Catholic parish had been established a year earlier as the first one east of the tracks of the New Jersey Railroad and Transportation Company. Its first pastor was the Reverend B. F. Allaire, formerly of Brooklyn, New York, beginning a direct succession that connected James Callan (1854-61), John M. Gervais (1861-73), and Patrick Cody (1873-1920). Bishop Bayley, a half-brother of Elizabeth Ann Seton – she who was destined for sainthood – was back again in July of 1863 for the installation of another cornerstone leading to completion of the construction.

Father Gervais played an exhaustive part in the work, helping to wheel stone to the high scaffolding and undertaking much physical labor. Construction went on for twelve years, the dedication finally taking place on June 17, 1866. Gothic in style, the church was embellished with dressed stone, buttresses, and, ultimately, a spire two hundred and twenty-five feet high that stood out prominently atop Newark's skyline. Among those participating in the dedication ceremony were New Jersey Governor Marcus L. Ward, a Newark native, and Bishop Bayley.

The successor to Father Gervais, the Reverend Patrick Cody, took over in 1873 to administer, for a long period extending into the twentieth century, a St. James complex that eventually included a school,

Rev. J. M. Gervais (top) and his successor at St. James Church, Rev. Patrick Cody (bottom).

St. Aloysius High School Class of 1925.

hospital, and convent complementing the church. The hospital was founded in 1900, its one hundred and five beds overseen by the Sisters of the Third Franciscan Order of Minor Conventuals, based in Syracuse, New York. The rectory was completed in 1903. As for the school program, it offered secondary as well as elementary levels for boys and girls.

St. Benedict's

Services organized especially for German immigrants were offered as early as 1838 in the basement of St. John's Church on Mulberry Street, the mother church for Roman Catholics in Newark. Then, in 1854, Benedictine clergy founded what became St. Benedict's Church (formally St. Benedictus), giving

Down Neck another Catholic parish alongside that of St. James.

A building was erected in 1857 at Barbara and Niagara streets, in an area that was home to many Catholic worshippers of German origin. It was destroyed by a storm of hurricane proportions. Succeeding it was a red-brick church, Romanesque in style and with a hundred-foot tower, that was dedicated in 1859.

St. Al's

The third Catholic parish east of the tracks in Newark was St. Aloysius Church, established in 1879 in classic "Neck" territory in the Twelfth Ward. Having started out as an appendage of St. James Church known as St. Thomas Mission, the church that came to be known familiarly as "St. Al's" put down permanent roots at Bowery and Freeman streets in an area that was inhabited by many residents of Irish origin.

The church building, a brownstone structure Gothic in style, was designed by Irish-born architect Jeremiah O'Rourke of Newark, with funds donated by the virtually adjacent Ballantine brewery. Dedication ceremonies were held on Sunday, May 8, 1881. The first pastor of St. Aloysius was the Reverend Walter M. Fleming. He guided the church's affairs until his death in 1892, and it was in his honor that Bowery Street was renamed Fleming Avenue – and out of a wish for disassociation with the skid-row reputation associated with the Bowery name that was being fostered in New York City.

Father Fleming once recalled, for a newspaper interview late in his life, what conditions were like earlier in his Down Neck career. He replied that the location of St. Aloysius was "marshy meadowland, irreclaimably irredeemable."

A Lithuanian Parish

Fulsome praise was expressed in a *Newark Sunday News* article on February 12, 1905, for the four-year-old Holy Trinity Church, a predominantly Lithuanian parish at 205 Adams Street in the Ironbound's Tenth Ward. Saluting parishioners for steadfast devotion to a communal cohesiveness of high order, the article asserted, in part:

One of the most remarkable instances of parochial prosperity in Newark is that of the Roman Catholic parish of the Holy Trinity in the Ironbound district … while there are less than 250 families … and none of them wealthy, within a year and a half the congregation has accumulated church property to the value of $25,000 … no big bequests, no liberal donations of large sums, and no unusual source of income, yet the little church and its congregation of workingmen and women have accomplished what many consider a marvel.

How it was done is perhaps best known to the rector, Rev. Vincent Stachniewicz, a young priest who scarcely knew a word of English when he assumed charge of the parish about a year and a half ago.

The parish had been started in 1894 as Sacred Heart of Jesus, its name changed soon thereafter to Holy Trinity. Eight lots on Adams Street, directly across from the tranquilly green area of East Side Park, were purchased in 1902. Before a church could be erected on Adams Street, parishioners attended services either at St. Stanislaus Church in central Newark or at Our Lady of Mount Carmel Church, the new Italian parish on Ferry Street.

Holy Trinity was started after many Lithuanians began taking up residence in the area of Adams and Warwick streets and New York Avenue. The pastor of exceptional ability, at the outset, was the Reverend W. V. Matulaitis. The initial church building was replaced by a handsome brick edifice of Romanesque design, its cornerstone laid in 1917. Five years later, the Lithuanian-born Reverend Ignatius Kelmelis began his long career as pastor.

The Basilica of the Ironbound

On a September in 1908, after Sunday Mass at St. Benedict's Church, worshippers of Polish origin in the Ironbound met to lay plans for a parish of their own. Out of this effort would arise St. Casimir's Church, one of the ornaments of the Roman Catholic Church in the Diocese of Newark.

Newark at the time had only one other Polish Catholic parish, St. Stanislaus, founded in 1889 and situated in center city. It was its pastor, in fact, who noted the growing Polish presence Down Neck and the feasibility of starting an additional parish there. At the 1908 meeting, a proposal was made by the Reverend Julius Manteuffel that a new parish be named after Casimir, the patron saint of Poland and Lithuania, which was approved. Parishioners then set their sights on erecting a combination church-school edifice.

The site ultimately chosen, at a meeting on November 1, 1908, was at Nichols and Tyler streets, and it is there that St. Casimir's Church was erected in a splendidly decorative style sufficient to win it recognition in years to come as "the basilica of the Ironbound." An initial structure, costing $35,000, was superseded by the grander one, accommodating the church sanctuary as a separate structure.

Assigned to head the fledgling parish, in February 1912, was a young, thirtyish Reverend Paul G. Knappek, who became a marathon-man legend. Construction began in 1917 and the church received its formal blessing on July 4, 1920, from Newark Bishop John J. O'Connor.

Majestic in design and decoration, the church – costing $190,000, a hefty burden for congregants of meager means – was Italian Renaissance in style. It boasted sumptuous frescoes and murals, handsome arches and gold-speckled ceilings, and exquisitely rendered stained-glass windows. Sharing the neighborhood spotlight with the adjacent East Side Commercial and Manual Training High School and with East Side Park, the St. Casimir complex – church, convent, school, and rectory – became the vital center of the Ironbound's Polish community.

In further recognition of the Polish and St. Casimir presence, the Newark City Commission in August of 1926 ordered the name of Tyler Street changed to honor Casimir Pulaski, the Polish nobleman-martyr of the American Revolutionary War.

St. Michael's

Easter Sunday in 1910 was an extra-special occasion for Greek Catholic worshippers in the Ironbound. Mass

St. Casimir Roman Catholic Church.

was celebrated for the first time at the new St. Michael's Russian Orthodox Church on Oliver Street. The orange-brick church, adorned by three brilliant gold onion domes, was situated on property directly across from East Side Park in the Tenth Ward. It was another symbol of the huge influx of immigrants from Eastern Europe – Ukrainians and Russians as well as Poles, Lithuanians, and others – to the industrial beehives of such urban centers as Newark. The parish was founded in 1906 by the Brotherhood of St. Michael, and the church's construction cost was borne by a congregation largely composed of working-class factory hands.

The church's address is 277 Oliver, near the intersection with Van Buren Street ultimately to stand as a neighbor with another Catholic landmark there, Our Lady of Mount Carmel Church, transplanted from its first site on McWhorter Street.

Also to arise in the area was St. George's Byzantine Catholic Church to serve the spiritual needs of Eastern Catholic worshippers. Congregants originally found space at 26 Houston, between Elm Road and New York Avenue, then erected a church of their own at 214 Warwick Street, between Pulaski and Lang streets.

St. George's was affiliated with the Byzantine Catholic Eparchy of Passaic. Guiding the parish in the early years was the Reverend George M. Kandra. A longtime pastor in the second half of the twentieth century was Monsignor Robert G. Moneta.

Congregation Thores Emes

In 1909, Orthodox Jews in the Ironbound held services in their new synagogue at 79 Jefferson Street, which was still undergoing construction. The synagogue was the spiritual home of Congregation Thores Emes ["Torah of Truth"], with nearly three hundred members in the opening period.

The opening services on Jefferson Street marked the start of the Jewish New Year 5670. Samuel Reiter was president of the congregation, its numbers including various merchants who operated businesses on Ferry Street, the neighborhood's main commercial artery, and at nearby locations that long were popular with local shoppers for their convenient access, making

STAINED-GLASS WINDOW OF SECOND REFORMED DUTCH CHURCH.

it unnecessary for trips to the major stores in Newark's central business district.

Familiar names locally were such as Steinberg, Nussbaum, and Goldfinger, all clothiers, and, a longtime presence at Congress and Lafayette streets, the pharmacist Meyer Olshin. As for the synagogue, it was fully built by 1911 – for three years previous to 1909, congregational events had been held at 142 Ferry Street.

Jews had begun settling in Newark steadily in the early 1880s as part of the great migration that brought waves of southern and central Europeans to American shores. There had been a smaller number of arrivals from various locales in the Old World, however, such as Louis Trier, who established a tannery on New Jersey Railroad Avenue after coming to Newark in 1844.

▪ ACHIEVERS ▪

Newark has had more than three dozen mayors since it became a city in 1836. Only four of them have come from the Down Neck / Ironbound neighborhood – Horace J. Poinier, Frederick C. Breidenbach, Ralph A. Villani, and Leo P. Carlin. Small as that number is, it suggests the range of multicultural diversity in the neighborhood's history.

Poinier was a lumber merchant who lived for a time at 50 Ferry Street. His ancestry was Huguenot – those Protestants of Calvinist tendency who left Catholic-dominated France in great numbers over religious differences. He was a founding member of the Sixth Presbyterian Church on Union Street, and when he became mayor in 1854 he strictly enforced the Sunday prohibition on consumption of alcoholic beverages.

Newark was afflicted at the time with an outbreak of cholera, which believers interpreted as God's punishment for failure to keep the Sabbath. In a locale that was home to so many beer-loving Germans, this was a prickly issue. The result was a conspicuous flow of traffic going back and forth on Sundays to East Newark, where drinking was permitted.

Poinier's lumber business was at 33 Commercial Street close to both the railroad tracks and the Passaic River. He was a Trustee of the Newark Fire Department, a founding member of the Howard Savings Institution, and, in his later years, President of the Newark City Insurance Company. His term as mayor was 1854 to 1857.

Breidenbach's ancestry was German – his father, Andrew, had been born in Bavaria. The Breidenbachs also belonged to the Sixth Presbyterian Church, but the younger Breidenbach took issue with those who wanted movie theatres closed on Sundays, arguing that this would be inequitable for so many Newark residents who lacked the financial means to own autos

LEFT: MAYOR RALPH A. VILLANI, SHOWN IN 1950 CUTTING INTO A HUGE PROVOLONE AT A NEWARK GROCERY STORE, WAS THE SON OF A DOWN NECK BUTCHER. HE SERVED AS NEWARK'S MAYOR FROM 1949 TO 1953. ABOVE: IRONBOUND BUSINESSMAN HORACE J. POINIER WAS MAYOR FROM 1854 TO 1857.

Mayor Leo P. Carlin served two terms, 1953–1962, defeating fellow Ironbound resident Ralph A. Villani in both elections.

family moved to Madison Street in the Ironbound, where the senior Villani had a butcher's shop for which the son made deliveries after school hours.

The young Villani (identified as "Raphael" in the 1910 Federal Census) attended Lafayette Street School and East Side High School and went on to Syracuse University and its law school. He became a municipal judge in 1933 and was elected to the Newark City Commission in 1941 and re-elected in 1945 and 1949, the year he was chosen as mayor by his fellow Commissioners.

As Commissioner of Parks and Public Property, Villani made his mark supervising the planting of thousands of trees around Newark, and he developed a city-wide "Learn to Swim" campaign focused on youths. Like many of Italian origin in pre-New Deal times, he was a Republican adherent, but he switched to the Democratic side in 1957. He had been defeated for the mayoralty by Leo P. Carlin in 1953, when Newark shifted from a Commission to a Mayor-Council form of government, and he lost again to Carlin in 1959. Villani's last hurrah came in 1962 with his election to the Newark City Council.

and thus could not easily visit the countryside for recreational purposes.

Fred Breidenbach was born Down Neck in 1876 and attended the Hamburg Place School. He had a photo studio at 172 Ferry Street for more than twenty years and lived nearby. He failed in a bid for a seat on the new City Commission that came into being in 1917, but then won election in 1921, moved to Newark's Weequahic section, and served as mayor from 1922 to 1925.

Villani, first of Newark's mayors to come from the city's large Italian-American population, served in that office from 1949 to 1953. He was born in Elizabeth in September, 1901, to Carmine and Anna Villani, immigrants from Avellino, east of Naples. The

Carlin's family lived on Fillmore Street in the Twelfth Ward. He attended St. Benedict's preparatory school, but had to leave to help support his large family. The head of a Teamsters union local, he served in the New Jersey State Assembly and was President of the Newark Board of Education. He was re-elected mayor in 1958 but lost in 1962 to U.S. Congressman Hugh J. Addonizio.

A Saintly Presence

The Ironbound can claim a relationship with a unique historical figure – the diminutive Italian nun who was elevated in 1946 to sainthood and world renown as Mother Cabrini. In 1899 she and her Missionary Sisters of the Sacred Heart – they became known as the Cabrini Nuns – started a parochial school for Italian immigrant children at Our Lady of Mount Carmel Church, at Ferry and McWhorter streets, and reputedly for a time in the basement of a factory building nearby.

The factory location is unspecified, but it seems noteworthy that the company headed by Bernard and James Shanley, labor contractors who made their fortune hiring countless numbers of Italians and others for railroad construction and maintenance, had office space during this period at Commerce and Market streets, across from the Pennsylvania Railroad tracks, at the location that became the site of a small area of greenery designated as Mother Cabrini Park.

It had been known as Ironbound Park, and the redesignation in honor of Frances Xavier Cabrini was the result of a petition drive headed by the Reverend Richard Caligaro, pastor of Our Lady of Mount Carmel Church. A resolution calling for the name change was then sponsored by Ralph A. Villani, the city's parks commissioner, and approved by the Newark City Council. The Cabrini Nuns left Newark in 1903 to undertake other works.

A Doctor's Prescription

The man credited with coining the Ironbound name, Dr. Herman C. H. Herold, was the subject of a testimonial banquet on the evening of March 3, 1904, attended by some two hundred and fifty friends and colleagues. The place was Harburger's Hall, at 82 Hamburg Place, and the banquet marked the physician-surgeon's fiftieth birthday and twenty-fifth year in the medical profession.

Herold was the longtime President of the Newark Board of Health and a participant in Republican activities Down Neck. Much praise was rendered that evening at Harburger's Hall, by such as Mayor Henry M. Doremus, for Dr. Herold's efforts in fighting the scourge of diphtheria and obtaining healthier drinking water for Newark residents. Herold, who lived on Congress Street next to Christ Episcopal Church, was active in campaign efforts, via the usual parades and mass rallies, to keep the popular President "Teddy" Roosevelt in the White House.

In 1888 Herold had been a delegate at the Republican National Convention in Chicago, and he was a delegate again in 1892 and 1904. In 1891 he was appointed by President William McKinley to become Collector of Internal Revenue for the Fifth District of New Jersey, and he retained that post until 1914.

Herold was the son of German-born emigrants, receiving his education at his father's German-English School and the Twelfth Ward Public School. His father had been a bookkeeper in an oilcloth factory at Market and Ferguson streets. Dr. Herold was graduated from New York's Bellevue Hospital Medical College in 1878. Upon his death in 1922, at his daughter's house in Newark's Weequahic section, Herold was praised in a *Newark Evening News* editorial for displaying "courage and resolution" in his various efforts for the public good, including acquiring the Pequannock Water Shed and thereby upgrading the city's drinking water, fighting the scourges of diphtheria and tuberculosis, and assisting in the establishment of Newark City Hospital (1882) and the Essex Mountain Sanatorium in Verona (1907). He also served on the Passaic Valley Sewerage Commission.

Looking Backward

By the end of his life span in 1905, William W. Morris had personally witnessed the transformation of Newark's east side from sparsely settled marshland to crowded industrial mecca. Born in New York City in 1830, Morris was still only an infant when he was brought to Newark and a house his father built on one of the new streets – at first called Harris, then Union – that had been carved out along Old Ferry Road. As he recalled in a 1901 newspaper article, the territory east of the newly installed New Jersey Railroad and Transportation Company line had become known locally as "Texas" owing to "its vast extent and its wilderness of swamps."

Morris, whose father was a founder of one of the earliest of Down Neck churches, Fifth Baptist, was a delegate to the Republican National Convention of 1860, in Chicago, that nominated Abraham Lincoln for the presidency. When Lincoln stopped at Newark on a snowy day in February, 1861, en route to his historic inauguration, Morris assisted as a military escort. He was an officer in the New Jersey state militia and member of a Newark branch of the Republican-leaning patriotic group known as the "Wideawakes." He and a cohort accompanied the President-elect's carriage along Broad Street to the South Park Presbyterian Church, where Lincoln gave a brief outdoor address before being conveyed to the Chestnut Street Depot on New Jersey Railroad Avenue and a waiting train for the next leg of his trip, to Trenton.

Morris attained the rank of major in the Union Army, serving under Generals Ambrose Burnside and Joseph Hooker at Fredericksburg and Chancellorsville, respectively, and at Gettysburg. He headed a veterans' battalion that helped quell the deadly draft riots in New York City in the summer of 1863 and helped carry out Lincoln's recruiting effort in New Jersey as the war dragged on.

Reflecting late in life on the incipient Ironbound of his boyhood days, he wrote: "In those early days there were no tall factory chimneys to belch smoke, and the whirr of machinery was unheard. The larger part of the tract consisted of farms and swamps. Nobody thought of living below the point formed by Ferry street and what is now known as Hamburg place, but which was then merely called the road to the meadows. There were scarcely a dozen streets then while now there are more than ten times that number."

A fervent Republican and amateur historian who was a member of the New Jersey Historical Society, Morris was a street commissioner in Newark and clerk of documents at the old City Hall. He died in August, 1905, after being struck by a horse-drawn delivery wagon at Broad and Market streets in downtown Newark.

Seeds of Invention

It may have been a relatively brief encounter that Thomas Alva Edison had with the neighborhood, but the area later to become recognized as the Ironbound nevertheless formed part of the backdrop that helped nurture Edison's inventive genius. He was a twenty-three-year-old Ohio product when, in February of 1870, he settled in Newark and set up shop on New Jersey Railroad Avenue.

Edison was associated there with his even younger partner, twenty-year-old William Unger, with whom he operated the Newark Telegraph Works at 15 New Jersey Railroad Avenue. The site, between Ferry and East Mechanic streets, was right across from the railway that soon was to be absorbed into the Pennsylvania Railroad system. Edison and Unger devoted themselves to the manufacture of improved "tickers" reporting the ups and downs of stock prices on the New York Stock Exchange.

Ultimately, East Mechanic Street (east of the railway) and Mechanic Street proper would be renamed Edison Place in his honor, and the site of Edison's first Newark venture would become part of a small greenery area, ultimately to be known as Peter Francisco Park (similar to Mother Cabrini Park – they flank either side of the triangular-shaped Ironbound Trust Company building).

Before he moved on, with his Newark bride, in 1876 to Menlo Park and his most famous inventions, Edison conducted business at three more sites on the eastern side of the New Jersey Railroad Avenue corridor, in addition to four other Newark locations. The areas on the eastern side touched, or were close to, Bruen, Green, Elm, and Oliver streets, and Edison also set up shop for a while in a place known as "White's Building" on the edge of the Morris Canal (later to become Raymond Boulevard) immediately east of the future Penn Station close to the Passaic River. (The inventor's Newark sites have been pinpointed by George J. Hill in his book *Edison's Environment: Invention and Pollution in the Career of Thomas Edison*, published by New Jersey Heritage Press.)

LEFT: THOMAS A. EDISON WITH A PHONOGRAPH, ONE OF HIS MOST SUCCESSFUL INVENTIONS. THE YOUNG INVENTOR WORKED AT SEVERAL DOWN NECK LOCATIONS EARLY IN HIS CAREER, FROM 1870 TO 1876.

The Dean of Prospect Street

The little church on Prospect Street ... and also on Congress Street. This was Christ Episcopal Church, a venerable brownstone sanctuary complemented by a red-brick rectory to its rear – and especially revered for its long association with the Reverend J. Nicholas Stansbury.

John Stansbury made his mark as Christ Church's rector, a stewardship that began on May 17, 1859, and lasted until 1891, when poor health caused his resignation. As an Episcopal dean, he was much revered for his sermons, his works – he was a founder of the charitable group that was the starting point for St. Barnabas Hospital – and his insistence that church membership be kept fully equitable, irrespective of any kind of financial consideration. His church at 76 Prospect Street, its origins dating to 1848, became known far and wide as "Stansbury's Church," and a parish house built in 1915 (the property extends from Prospect to Congress) became a memorial designated as Stansbury Hall.

Born in Baltimore in 1833, Dean Stansbury was ordained by Protestant Episcopal Bishop George Washington Doane in 1859 – Doane's last ordination, just prior to his death. Stansbury himself died in Newark on May 28, 1892.

Early Promise

The man who almost became President spent part of his formative years Down Neck, revealing a touch of future glory. He was "Charlie" Hughes, and he ranked first in his graduating class at the Tenth Ward Grammar School, on Oliver Street, in 1873. He was destined, as Republican candidate Charles Evans Hughes, to nearly unseat President Woodrow Wilson in 1916.

He was the son of the Reverend David C. Hughes, pastor of the Fifth Baptist Church, directly across from Lafayette Street School. The younger Hughes, whose family lived in the church parsonage at 164 Elm Street, went on to Newark High School for less than a year of study before the family relocated to New York City. Before he was enrolled in the Oliver Street school, "Charlie" Hughes briefly attended the Fifth Ward Grammar School – later to be titled officially as

THE SON OF A DOWN NECK PASTOR, CHARLES EVANS HUGHES SPENT HIS YOUTH IN THE IRONBOUND BEFORE THE FAMILY MOVED TO NEW YORK, WHERE HE LATER SERVED AS GOVERNOR. HE RAN AGAINST, AND NEARLY UNSEATED, PRESIDENT WOODROW WILSON IN 1916. HE WAS APPOINTED SECRETARY OF STATE IN 1921 AND CHIEF JUSTICE OF THE UNITED STATES IN 1930.

Lafayette Street School. The Hughes family had been in Newark since 1869, the year the school on Oliver Street was opened.

Hughes became Governor of New York State and Chief Justice of the United States. During the period when he set his sights, in vain, on capturing the White House, he fondly recalled in a newspaper interview his Newark school days, especially those spent on Oliver Street under the tutelage of Mrs. Joseph A. Halleck, wife of the school's principal.

Grand Designs

John H. Ely was born in New Hope, Pennsylvania, but it was in Newark that he made his name as an architect of distinction – and Down Neck where he made his residence for many years. Settling in Newark in 1882, he started out as a carpenter – he is listed as such in the city directory of 1884-85 while residing at 138 Congress Street – and he went on to design many prominent Newark buildings.

With his son, Wilson C. Ely, joining him, the Ely firm designed a number of landmarks, including Newark City Hospital, the National Newark & Essex Banking Company, Mutual Benefit Life, the Firemen's Insurance Company, East Orange City Hall, Morristown Memorial Hospital, The Ironbound Trust Company, and, most famously, Newark City Hall.

The latter building, exemplifying the classic lines of the Beaux-Arts style in sync with the City Beautiful impulse of the early twentieth century, was perhaps Ely's crowning achievement. It took years to build and cost two million dollars. The new City Hall was dedicated on a snowy Thursday in December of 1906 with speeches by Mayor Henry M. Doremus and Mayor-elect Jacob Haussling.

The Ely works also include a three-story training stable and repair shop for the Newark Fire Department, at 56 Prospect Street in the Ironbound (directly across from the Portuguese Sport Club), that was considered exceptional for the training of horses for fire service and their care in the event of illness, a building which at the time was reputed to be "the finest and most substantial building of its kind in the country." It was opened in May of 1909.

ARCHITECTS JOHN H. ELY (TOP) AND HIS SON WILSON C. ELY (BOTTOM) DESIGNED SUCH LANDMARK STRUCTURES AS NEWARK CITY HALL AND THE IRONBOUND TRUST COMPANY.

The Newark directory also shows Ely and his wife, Lydia, residing at two other locations in their Ironbound years, 116 Union Street and 170 Lafayette Street.

A Pair of Guiding Lights

It could be said that the end of an era was truly reached on July 11, 1920, with the death of the longtime pastor of St. James Church, the Reverend Patrick Cody. At the age of eighty-two, Monsignor Cody was a pillar of this mostly Irish haven, guiding the affairs of a complex that included church, school, hospital, and convent from his rectory office at 250 Lafayette Street, corner of Jefferson.

He had been pastor since 1873 of this grandest of the Ironbound's places of worship. He oversaw completion of the construction of the church and its prominent steeple in addition to the other buildings.

Father Cody was born in Tipperary, Ireland, in 1839. He was a cousin of "Buffalo Bill" Cody, the famed Western hero and peripatetic showman who is said to have visited on a couple of occasions at the St. James rectory on Lafayette Street. In December of 1863, Cody and a fellow Seton Hall seminarian were the first priests ordained at that Roman Catholic school's new campus in South Orange. He served for a time as a young Vice-President of Seton Hall, and in 1913 the Church conferred on him the rank of Monsignor.

In 1919, a year before Cody's death, a young priest named Matthew J. Toohey, who had also been trained at Seton Hall, became assistant pastor at St. James. He would soon be off to hold other assignments before the Diocese called for him to return to St. James in 1934, at the age of forty-five, to become its pastor, a post he would fill until his death in 1948.

Born in Hoboken, Father Toohey was one of twelve children. He served in France as a United States Army chaplain during World War I, and years later he became national chaplain of the Catholic War Veterans. During his tenure at St. James, the parochial school was enlarged and recreational activities increased. In the largely working-class and heavily "ethnic" ambience of this Down Neck area, the school was prized by many among the Catholic faithful as a kind of semi-privileged enclave.

Toohey was something of an Ironbound booster – Jefferson Street, a central part of his domain, was sometimes known as "the Irish Fifth Avenue." At the same time, he was a fierce anti-communist who vociferously supported the controversial efforts of Jersey City's powerful Mayor Frank Hague to suppress public displays of "Red" activity in his municipal fiefdom. In 1938, Father Toohey attracted wide notoriety for complaining that the University of Newark was "honey-combed with radicals of the most extreme type," criticism that helped to bring down its chief administrator.

A Lifetime of Service

The Reverend Julius H. Wolff was long associated with Hamburg Place, the home (at its intersection with Ann Street) of the Third German Presbyterian Church he had guided since way back in 1875. So it must have

Vasco de Sousa Jardim, the author's father, emigrated to the United States in 1920 from the Portuguese island of Madeira. He settled initially in Massachusetts, where he found work as a newspaper reporter and printer.

In 1928 he moved with his young wife Angelina to Newark. He set up a printing shop in the Ironbound district and worked for the newly established Portuguese-language Luso-Americano newspaper, which, due to the Depression, folded some years later. Sensing an opportunity, Jardim took over the publication in 1939 and served as publisher and editor for 40 years. At his retirement in 1979, he was widely regarded as the dean of Portuguese-American journalism. The Luso-Americano remains in publication to this day.

Jardim also distinguished himself as a civic leader within Newark's Portuguese-American community. He was one of the founders of the Luso-American Fraternal Association, member and officer of the Portuguese Sport Club, Saint Anthony Society, Portuguese-American Citizens Club, and Sport Maritimo Murtoense, and appointee to Newark's first Human Relations Commission in 1952.

Among his many distinctions was being named recipient of Portugal's foremost civilian honor, the Prince Henry medal, in 1965, for his journalistic and fraternal efforts on behalf of his fellow immigrants.

been a bit jarring when Hamburg Place as a street address was dropped, abruptly, for a presumably more politically correct "Wilson Avenue" in the World War I period beset by anti-German sentiment. Wolff, at least, didn't have to suffer the change for too long; he died on November 18 at his home on … Wilson Avenue. (The change had taken effect just a few months earlier.)

At the beginning of Reverend Wolff's tenure as pastor, services were held in a small chapel at Madison and Ferry streets. It was in 1882 that the church relocated to Ann Street at Hamburg Place. A parsonage was built there the following year for Dr. Wolff and his wife, Louise, and a building for Sunday school instruction was added in 1891, to be enlarged in 1895.

Born in upstate New York, Julius H. Wolff was a member of the first graduating class at the German Theological Seminary, which became Bloomfield Theological Seminary and then Bloomfield College. The school in 1909 conferred on him an honorary degree of doctor of divinity. As a young man, Reverend Wolff did

WILLIAM HARRIGAN WAS DOWN NECK'S
MOST INFLUENTIAL POLITICAL FIGURE
DURING THE LATE 19TH AND EARLY 20TH
CENTURIES.

the children of immigrant families at Our Lady of Mount Carmel Church in the Ironbound. Thus did Father D'Aquila help to organize the first Italian parochial school in Newark, with help from the fabled Mother Cabrini.

A trained musician and accomplished organist, D'Aquila raised the cultural level of the parish during his pastorate of thirty-nine years. He was only twenty-four when he left behind his native Campobasso province for Newark to become Mount Carmel's second pastor, in 1894, an appointee of Bishop Winand Wigger.

Father Ernesto was raised to the rank of monsignor during the pontificate of Pius XI. He also for a time administered the affairs of another Italian parish in the Ironbound, Our Lady of the Holy Rosary, at 179 Emmet Street. His major achievement came in working with a later Bishop, Thomas J. Walsh, in securing property on Oliver Street, in the Ironbound's Tenth Ward, as a more appropriate site for a parochial school, removed from the encroaching commercial and industrial activity that engulfed the original church location at Ferry and McWhorter streets. It was clear to the monsignor that the center of gravity for his parishioners in terms of residential and social life style was shifting toward the Ironbound's interior, with Independence Park as a kind of centerpiece. Father D'Aquila died on May 8, 1933, in Newark.

missionary work in lower Manhattan. He was stated clerk of the Presbytery of Newark for many years. In tribute to the long stewardship of this Ironbound icon, the congregation of Third German Presbyterian in 1936 did a name switch of its own – officially becoming Wolff Memorial Presbyterian Church.

Looking Ahead

It was a young priest not long out of Italy, the Reverend Ernesto D'Aquila, who helped facilitate the importation of nuns from his native country to educate and nurture

Marathon Man

In both a community and a profession marked by unusually lengthy terms of service to the faithful, the Reverend Paul G. Knappek stands out in bold relief. As a young, thirtyish novice of Polish origin, Father Knappek came to Newark in February of 1912 to head a fledgling Roman Catholic parish in a community peopled predominantly by his fellow nationals.

The goal was of course a church of their own, and Father Knappek no doubt worked hard to raise the necessary funds among an immigrant people not blessed with financial resources. The end result was a magnificent St. Casimir's Church on the future Pulaski Street. Construction began in 1917, and the church received its formal blessing on July 4, 1920, with Bishop John J. O'Connor of the Newark Diocese officiating.

Father Knappek, elevated by the Vatican to the rank of Monsignor, served a stewardship at St. Casimir's that lasted for an exceptional fifty-two years. He died, aged eighty-seven, on May 5, 1964, at St. James Hospital.

A Political Legend

Of all those who left a mark on the Ironbound's history, probably no one stands taller as a larger-than-life personality than William Harrigan.

They called him any number of names, mostly endearing – Uncle Bill, Old Bill, The Old Man, The Old War Horse. He more or less ruled the political roost for a good part of the event-filled period that stretched from the eighteen-eighties until the Progressive years when this feisty Democratic "boss" was brushed aside by reformers of the Woodrow Wilson stripe.

In strident marches through the Ironbound, loyalists and ward-heelers waved high the banners and bunting of the William Harrigan Association, based in the Twelfth Ward, as it flaunted its ballot-box capabilities at rally after rally around the turn of the century.

Following his emigration as a child from Ireland – he was born on October 31, 1838, in County Dublin – Harrigan received a grade-school education in his new land. He worked as a trucker and then a horse dealer in Newark before embarking on a successful business career as a manufacturer of mineral waters. His sociable geniality led him naturally into the political realm, and he served for a number of years, starting in 1883, in the New Jersey State Assembly, was a delegate to the Democratic National Conventions of 1884 and 1888, an alderman on the Newark Common Council, and the city's police commissioner.

Among several other reforms, he pushed as a legislator for establishment of what became East Side Park in the Ironbound's Tenth Ward and construction of a much-needed sewer line through eastern Newark in pursuit of improved sanitation and health measures, and he made it a crime for railroad companies not to maintain gates and flagmen at street crossings.

In his successful bid for election as Sheriff of Essex County in 1908, Harrigan's shrewd utilization of a George M. Cohan hit song from a Broadway musical helped propel him to victory. On the evening of August 20, his supporters turned out by the hundreds to parade through the streets of the Ironbound. It is estimated, the *Newark Evening News* reported, "that fully 2,000 men were in line when the parade left Bowery and Market streets [the Harrigan clubhouse was at 645 Market] and all along the route followed by the marchers the friends of the 'Old Warhorse' fell in line, swelling the number in the procession to about 2,500."

Riding in a horse-drawn barouche, Harrigan led them on, and a hundred or so youthful singers accompanied a marching band in boisterous renditions of the Broadway ditty "H-A-double R-I-G-A-N spells Harrigan."

Amid bonfires and fireworks, the paraders strutted along the streets – Bowery, Ferry, Niagara, Barbara, Hamburg Place, back to Ferry and on to Prospect, Pacific, East Kinney, Jefferson, and Market, ending up at a favored saloon, Bitz's Hall, at 4 Bowery Street, for refreshments. The brassy political spectacle inspired a teasing headline in the Republican-leaning *News*: "EVERY ONE FOR / H-A-RR-I-G-A-N."

Harrigan's last hurrah was precipitated by his ill-considered bid in 1910 to become the Democratic nominee for Governor of New Jersey. He proved no match for the rising star that was Woodrow Wilson. Harrigan, who lived at 42 Fillmore Street, died in 1920. Mourners attended a Solemn High Mass of Requiem celebrated at St. James Church in his behalf.

Stirred Up

Another important political figure of that era with Ironbound connections was John F. Monahan, an alderman and longtime Democratic leader in the Fifth Ward. Monahan, whose Down Neck addresses included Market Street and Jefferson Street, bucked a reform-minded Republican tide to win election as Sheriff of Essex County in 1911. The electioneering flavor of the time is reflected in the following *Newark Evening News* notice of October 27, 1911:

> The William Harrigan Association and the John F. Monahan Association will unite in stirring up the "Ironbound District" for the Democratic ticket tonight. Harrigan people will march from their headquarters at 645 Market street to the Monahan headquarters on East Mechanic street [the future Edison Place] and then the combined forces with bands and drum corps, will parade the Fifth, Tenth and Twelfth wards. After the parade an indoor meeting. The demonstration promises to be the largest seen in the "Ironbound District" since the big Harrigan meeting and parade three years ago.

Six years later, in an historic election, Monahan was one of five men chosen by voters to manage municipal affairs as Newark broke with its past and embarked on a different form of government – a City Commission. Monahan, who in the process became Commissioner of Parks and Public Property, served on the governing body with former Mayor Thomas L. Raymond, Alexander Archibald, Charles P. Gillen, and William J. Brennan, a onetime Ballantine brewery worker whose son would win fame as a Justice on the Supreme Court of the United States.

AN ILLUSTRATED MAP OF NEWARK IN 1916 SHOWS THE (ODDLY SHADED) IRONBOUND DISTRICT ALONG THE S-SHAPED CURVE OF THE PASSAIC RIVER AS IT FLOWS THROUGH THE MEADOWLANDS OF NEWARK BAY.

CREDITS

About the Author

Edward A. Jardim was born in Newark, New Jersey, in 1932. He resided for most of his early years on Ferry Street in the city's Ironbound district, where his father published a Portuguese-language weekly newspaper, the *Luso-Americano*. He graduated from East Side High School in 1950 and studied journalism at Temple University in Philadelphia, with time out for service in the U.S. Army.

Mr. Jardim has had a long editorial career at a number of publications, including the *New York Daily News* and

The author, Edward A. Jardim (at left), with his mother Angelina, sister Natalie, and brother Vasco outside the offices of the Luso-Americano newspaper on Ferry Street in Newark, circa 1944.

other journals. He and his wife, the former Joy Menza – her grandparents were among the earliest Italian immigrants to settle in the Ironbound – are longtime residents of New Jersey's Long Hill Township, where they raised their six children.

Acknowledgments

Getting familiar with a neighborhood, its character and how it got that way involves a good bit of snooping around. So it's helpful to be operating in a place like New Jersey with its rather fulsome supply of historical archives. Places like the New Jersey State Library and the State Archives, in Trenton, the Rutgers University libraries and the New Jersey Historical Society and beyond.

But of course the source par excellence for inquiries into the Ironbound district and its development is the Newark Public Library. On that subject, the place is a treasure trove, its files plentiful – in print and on microfilm and in whatever form – for newspaper articles going quite a way back in time, in books and maps and photos and directories. The heart of it all, up on the Library's third floor, is the New Jersey Information Center (NJIC) – now formally named for its longtime director, Charles F. Cummings.

He's gone now, but associates and staffers persist with the same degree of patience and helpfulness that he exemplified. We were most fortunate, in our own research, to brush up with such as Cummings and two other sympatico figures especially knowledgeable about

Newark and its environs and their history – John T. Cunningham and Clement Price – now also departed but much missed.

We owe an additional debt of gratitude for assistance with photo research to George S. Hawley, Ph.D., and Tom Anker of the Newark Public Library; Paul Matinho and Natalie Matinho of the *Luso-Americano*; and Paul J. Kiell, M.D., who provided the cover image.

Photo Credits
bigmapblog.com 8

Coppermine Photo Gallery 17

Essex County, N.J., Illustrated, Press of L. J. Hardham, Newark, N. J., 1897 54, 59, 61T, 61B, 73T, 73B, 74

Courtesy of Paul J. Kiell, M.D. front cover

Jim Kuhn/Flickr, licensed under CC BY 2.0 28 (top), 28 (bottom)

Library of Congress 7, 9, 14, 21, 22, 25, 26, 29, 30, 32T, 32B, 50L, 50R, 70, 73, 78-9

Courtesy of Natalie Matinho 47, 49, 75, 80

Newark Public Library 4, 6, 11, 17, 36, 37, 38T, 38B, 39, 40, 43, 52, 56, 58, 62, 65L, 65R, 66, 68, 76, back cover

Newark Public Library/ Rutgers University Community Repository/Courtesy of The Mastakas Family 20

Newark Public Library Special Collections 34, back cover

New Jersey Historical Society/Rutgers University Community Repository 18

New York Public Library Digital Collection 41, 46, 48

New York Public Library, Lionel Pincus and Princess Firyal Map Division 2

Design and Layout
Laura Wilson, John Gattuso, and Giovanna Gattuso at Gattuso Media Design.

For information about custom book publishing or to inquire about a deluxe hardcover edition of this book, please contact us at:

Gattuso Media Design
P.O. Box 481
Frenchtown, NJ 08825
john@gattusomediadesign.com
gattusomediadesign.com

To inquire about wholesale discounts or for information about custom book publishing, including a deluxe hardcover edition of this book, please contact us at:

Stone Creek Publications, Inc.
c/o Gattuso Media Design
P.O. Box 481
Frenchtown, NJ 08825
e-mail: john@gattusomediadesign.com
tel: 908-996-1020

Buy additional copies of this book at
www.ironboundbook.com or
www.amazon.com.

Made in the USA
San Bernardino, CA
06 May 2016